TOXIC SCHOOLING:

How Schools Became Worse

by Clive Harber

Educational Heretics Press

Published 2009 by Educational Heretics Press
113 Arundel Drive, Bramcote, Nottingham NG9 3FQ

Copyright © 2009 Educational Heretics Press

British Cataloguing in Publication Data

Harber, Clive
    Toxic Schooling:
    How schools became worse

ISBN   978-1-900219-37-2

Design and production: Educational Heretics Press

Cover design by Educational Heretics Press

Printed by
    Adlard Print Ltd., Ruddington, Nottingham

Contents

Introduction   1

Chapter 1   The School That I'd Like
            Edward Blishen   9

Chapter 2   Pedagogy of the Oppressed
            Paulo Freire   16

Chapter 3   Compulsory Mis-Education
            Paul Goodman   22

Chapter 4   The Betrayal of Youth
            James Hemming   29

Chapter 5   How Children Fail
            John Holt   36

Chapter 6   Deschooling Society
            Ivan Illich   41

Chapter 7   Life in Classrooms
            Philip Jackson   48

Chapter 8   Education and Ecstacy
            George Leonard   52

Chapter 9   The Little Red Schoolbook
            Soren Hansen and
            Jasper Jensen   57

Chapter 10 Education for Self-Reliance
Julius Nyerere   **62**

Chapter 11 Teaching as a Subversive
Activity
Neil Postman and Charles
Weingartner   **64**

Chapter 12 School is Dead
Everett Reimer   **71**

Chapter 13 Freedom to Learn
Carl Rogers   **76**

Chapter 14 Key Critiques   **85**

Chapter 15 Schooling Today
- Much the Same?   **87**

Chapter 16 Schooling Today
- Making Matters Worse?   **112**

Chapter 17 What Is To Be Done?   **140**

References   **151**

Further Reading   **165**

Introduction

Love Teaching: Hate School?

If you are an excellent teacher who really cares about student success, and are looking for a better way to teach, then consider this: **Kip McGrath** business owners set their own hours, decide who they will tutor, have almost no paperwork, effect positive changes on students, have no discipline worries, enjoy great relations with parents, earn very good incomes and run their own professional tutoring centres from commercial premises.

Best Of All It's Not Like School

(Advert)

In June 2008 *The Times* newspaper (24/6) published a letter addressed to Dr.Tanya Byron from two parents whose daughter was behaving badly at school and then refused to attend. The parents explained it by adolescence, peer pressure and, after discussion with the school counsellor, being an only child. Their GP referred them to the local child and adolescent mental health service of the NHS. They were told to make life as uncomfortable as possible at home for the daughter to coax her back to school. They eventually moved to another school but she again refused to attend. The letter ends with the statement *"The problem is obviously not with the school..."*, although no reason is given for this statement. The reply from Dr.Tanya Byron describes school refusal as a 'known disorder'. That the nature of school itself might be a problem is not acknowledged, though she does mention incidental 'school-related' problems such as bullying and lack of friends. The recommendation is that the daughter should see a private clinical psychologist who specialises in 'treating' school refusal. What is interesting is that throughout the whole correspondence the institution of school is treated a natural, unquestioned and given 'good'. There is not a hint that school itself may be part of the problem. This is just one small example of how schooling has come to be regarded as an inevitable and beneficial aspect of society.

Every year the United Nations Development Programme (UNDP) produces a book called the *Human Development Report.* This is perhaps the most authoritative international statement on issues surrounding human development. In this annual publication the UNDP ranks all the countries of the world from 1 to 177 according to a wide range of variables but special emphasis is laid on what they term the 'Human Development Index'. This is a composite index of what they consider to be the four key indicators of human development. These are life expectancy at birth, the adult literacy rate, wealth per capita and, most important for present purposes, the combined enrolment rates for primary, secondary and tertiary levels of formal education. Thus it is again assumed that enrolment in formal education, schooling, is necessarily and inherently a 'good thing', that it is a key indicator of development and that what happens inside schools and higher education is automatically of benefit to both individuals and society. This assumption is shared, most of the time, by national governments, global institutions like the World Bank and international aid agencies, where the dominant concern is with access to schooling rather than what happens in schooling. This is reflected in the enormous global expenditure on formal education and the major conference held at Jomtien, Thailand in 1990 when most governments of the world met to plan how they would provide universal primary education for all children by the year 2000. This was followed by a similar enormous conference held in

Dakar, Senegal in 2000 where they met again to explain why they had not achieved their targets for 2000 but would do so by 2015. Globally, there is far more concern with rights *to* education than rights *in* education because formal education is perceived in an overwhelmingly positive light.

In fact, there are three ways of looking at the relationship between schooling and society, all of which have some truth in them but not all of which have equal significance in debates on education. First, is the dominant discourse in international debates on education – that education is of significant benefit both to the individual and society. This can be, for example, economic benefit in the form of human capital theory where education increases the employment skills, productivity and earning power of individuals and hence contributes to economic growth and equality of opportunity. Or education might contribute socially and politically by developing the values and behaviours required for a suitable political culture that will help to sustain a democratic political system (see, for example, Harber and Davies 1997). These sorts of benefit of education are taken for granted by many in education and in the wider society and political system, hence the huge public and private expenditure on education internationally and the huge international educational effort to achieve primary education for all by 2015.

The second, less heard, discourse, is that of schooling as reproduction which challenges human capital theory's notion that education enables equal opportunities for all. Instead, while seemingly opening up opportunity for all and contributing to the development of an economic and social system based on open competition, achievement and merit, in fact the education system merely serves to reproduce things as they are. Children from poor backgrounds go to poor schools and then into poorly paid, low status jobs or unemployment. A small number of children from poor backgrounds succeed and this provides the appearance of a meritocratic system whereas in reality it merely serves to mask the role of education in perpetuating and reproducing inequality.

The third discourse, not heard about much at all, is that schooling not only reproduces society fundamentally as it is but also actively makes the lives of individuals worse and harms the wider society. This is because schools, far from consistently and uniformly being institutions of care and protection in fact both reproduce and cause violence. Not only do they not necessarily protect pupils from different forms of violence in the wider society but they actively perpetrate violence on pupils themselves.

This book is concerned with the second and third of these relationships between schooling and society and particularly with the third. Despite the overwhelmingly positive gloss put on schools by international agencies, the media, politicians and many in education itself, the reality, though much less discussed, is that disaffection with the profoundly negative features of schooling is global and can manifest itself in a number of ways – active and aggressive resistance within school, official exclusion resulting from resistance, passive resistance/non-cooperation, mental truancy, actual truancy, temporary or permanent drop out (especially in countries where formal education is not universal); school 'phobia' and the adoption of alternative modes of education such as home-based education. Yoneyama (2000) provides a useful analysis of four explanatory discourses that inform the debate on 'Tokokyohi' or school phobia in Japan. Three out of four - the psychiatric discourse (mental illness), the behavioural discourse (pupil laziness) and the socio-medical discourse (pupil fatigue) - blame pupils and their parents for not fitting into school. School is the default position, a given good. An example of this approach was a report on school behaviour and disaffection by the English Office for Standards in Education (OFSTED) in 2005 which found that schools faced particular problems with children aged four to six who are 'ill-prepared socially and emotionally' for school and that many disruptive pupils have special needs, poor language skills or come from disadvantaged or dysfunctional families (Slater 2005).

However, Yoneyama's fourth discourse, the citizens' discourse, regards school phobia and other forms of school refusal as the normal response of normal students – it is the schools that are sick, students are not sick. For example, a study of 'hidden drop-out' in schools in Albania, where many children simply survive in schools by unobtrusively going through the motions without any real engagement or learning, found that whereas teachers blamed parents, students and resources, in reality it was the constant, authoritarian whole-class instruction supported by behavioural control based on admonition and reproach that was the real problem. It was more a case of push-out than drop-out   (Sultana 2006). Perhaps the one in twenty pupils in Britain that now suffer from 'school phobia' (TES 12/9/2008) have simply understood better. It is also interesting to note that children labelled as 'schoolphobic' tend to be of 'average or above average intelligence, with a good social conscience (Moore 2002). This book is concerned with Yoneyama's fourth discourse – the role that school plays internationally in perpetrating disaffection because of the very nature of schooling itself.

Unease with schooling is not new:

"We are faced by the paradoxical fact that education has become one of the chief obstacles to intelligence and freedom of thought" (Bertrand Russell 1926, from *On Education* P.28)

In the late nineteenth and early twentieth centuries a variety of those concerned with education – Edmond

Holmes, A.S.Neill, Rudolf Steiner, Margaret McMillan, Charlotte Mason, Susan Isaacs and Bertrand Russell (Stanbrook 2002) - were critical of schooling and suggested more personalised, democratic and humane forms of education as alternatives. However, in the 1960s and 1970s, a period of social and cultural upheaval in the West and political change caused by decolonisation in many developing countries, a number of writers again began to question and critique the relevance and benevolence of schooling. This book examines the main ideas in a dozen or so key texts on schooling produced roughly during the period 1960 to 1980. For reasons of space, a selection it had to be, as there were other important books produced during the period that are not considered here. No doubt my own history and preferences have played a role in this selection as I was a pupil, student teacher, teacher and teacher educator during this period and read most of the texts at the time. This book then examines the extent, if any, to which these critiques had an effect on changing and improving the nature of schooling provided today or whether in some ways the situation is actually worse.

Sadly, and somewhat puzzlingly, women are missing from the authors reviewed and even those left out. In the early part of the twentieth century their presence in writing on radical critiques of schooling was clear, as is evident from the list cited above. This may have something to do with the post-war role of women in public and professional life but I will have to leave that to the historians to investigate. What was clear, re-reading the texts was the presence of what would now be considered sexist language – the ubiquitous use of he/him/his. I have tried to avoid this in my summaries of the books.

The books reviewed are primarily, though not exclusively, based on American and British experience. However, while context may cause varieties in certain aspects of schooling such as levels of resources and professionalism and the degree and severity of authoritarianism, there is also much about the structure, content and processes of contemporary schooling that remains much the same whatever the context. This is because of the historical origins and purposes of schooling and the way that it has spread around the globe (Alexander 2000; Harber 2004; Harber and Davies 1997). The discussion following the synopses of the books on how applicable the critiques are to schooling uses evidence and commentary on both England, where the writer is based, and a wider international context.

What is obvious is that, globally, the basic model of schooling critiqued in these books – a set curriculum, blocks of time devoted to separate subjects, competitive tests and examinations, pupil membership of classes with the teacher in control, bureaucratic organisation, a set of buildings that pupils and staff come to every day, the link to qualifications, the emphasis on answers rather than questions and issues – remains essentially the same. Visit almost any country in the world and go to a school and, despite superficial variations, you will recognise the basic elements instantly. It was this model that the writers reviewed in this book were critical of and it is the contemporary applicability of their criticisms that is discussed in more depth in the latter part of the book.

All debate about education is fundamentally political because it concerns the ultimate questions of what sort of people and societies we are trying to create. For these writers there was a large gap between schooling and the type of education required in a genuinely democratic society. However, for others an education based on control, tradition, the learning of 'facts' and uniformity is actually a good thing because of the type of political system and citizen that are considered desirable. It is the contention of this book that in reality, despite some exceptions and with some modifications, the latter practice of schooling remains strongly dominant, and in some ways has actually strengthened, over the three or four decades since these trenchant critiques were published. For someone like myself who agrees with many of the criticisms of schools made in these books, and who is nearing the end of his professional career in education, this is a sad and depressing conclusion. So I will end the introduction with a joke.

A female educationalist who is critical of schools dies and goes to heaven (a bit odd as the educationalist is also an atheist). God says to her that she can ask him any question and it will be answered truthfully. She asks God, *"Will schools ever be replaced by a more humane, happy and democratic form of learning?"*, to which God replies that there is some good news and bad news. *"The good news is yes, schools will be replaced. The bad news is, not in my lifetime".*

Chapter one

The School that I'd Like
by Edward Blishen
(Harmonsworth:Penguin, 1969)

"Schools usually have one thing in common - they are institutions of today run on the principles of yesterday" (15 year-old girl).

"I am tired of hearing that the hope of my country lies in my generation. If you give me the same indoctrination as a child, how can you expect me to be any different from you?" (15 year-old girl).

This book summarises the outcomes of a competition held by *The Observer* newspaper in December 1967 when British secondary school pupils were asked to describe 'the school that I'd like'. There were over a thousand entries. Blishen felt that, in the main and with the exception of the minority of cases when teachers had clearly directed the exercise, the answers were responsible and serious but that,

"the radical note that was so pervasive was astonishingly steady, reasonable and supported by instances. I've never read so much that was so full of complaints and criticisms, of schemes for imaginative innovation, and yet that was, as a whole, very sober".

The picture that emerged was one of children being told what to do and how to do it:

"The picture they build up of learning as it now most often is in the schools is one in which they, the pupils, are passive, sometimes very reluctant recipients; the teachers are the providers – aided, if that is the word, by textbooks that also, oppressively if not dully, provide. It is this pattern of passively receiving,

magisterially providing, that the children worry away at".

The children want to find out things for themselves:

"From all quarters of the educational scene it comes, this expression of children's longing to take upon themselves some of the burden of deciding what should be learnt, how it should be learnt...above all, to learn by talking, debating with the teacher as a senior confederate rather than the sole provider...they want to discover how to be responsible for themselves and their own ideas".

Many of the respondents had good memories of their primary schools where, unlike secondary schools, active learning and discovery played bigger roles. While the respondents were generally kind about teachers in terms of their low pay and burdensome administrative duties, they were also critical of attachment to trivial rules and failure to admit ignorance or uncertainty. And schools, they said, should be happy places.

Some of the key themes that emerged and which Blishen draws attention to in his introduction were:

- They wanted school buildings to be more comfortable and interesting with common rooms in which they could relax.
- Examinations were seen as the root of all evil, causing remote relationships with teachers and formalising teacher-centred classrooms.
- Many were against timetables as a set of tiny boxes with each subject in a box and there was great hatred of bells which artificially divided up time and did not correspond with moments of interest and matters that need to be pursued.
- A minority wanted to abandon school uniform altogether, though the majority wanted to

make it brighter and more responsive to changes in fashion.

- There was widespread rejection of religious assemblies and religious instruction as a form of indoctrination – though the comparative study of religion and debates on moral issues were supported.
- But standing out above everything else was the children's desire to teach themselves – 'The children seem to sense that you enter the world of the late twentieth century ill-armed if all you have done is to submit, to some degree or other, to a predetermined, pinched, examination-harried course of instruction from which in its nature most of the excitement and surprise of learning are excluded'.
- They want to take risks, intellectually and emotionally, and are critical of the education system for lacking any kind of courage.
- The girls were most vehemently opposed to single sex schools.

In his introduction to the rest of the book, which is largely made up entirely of quotations from the young people who responded, Blishen finally comments that,

"When I was reading these essays, the image of the prison returned to me again and again. We imprison the courage and the curiosity of our children".

Blishen divides the books into a series of sections according to the main themes he saw as emerging. The first, entitled, *The Key to Life is Flexibility* could almost sum up the book with its strongly critical quotations on the boredom of the rigid and regimented nature of school, often backed up by corporal punishment. There is a palpable desire in this chapter and others for greater freedom and variety. One pupil simply says, *"I don't think I would get on very well in my ideal school because I am too used to being told what to do",* whereas another simply notes that the school that he would like, he already has, because he is being educated at home.

Other themes that emerge from the remaining quotations are:
- the need for more education to take place at first hand and on a more experiential basis outside of the classroom,
- the importance of discussing current social and political issues in school,
- that schools should provide an equal chance for all and your chance of success or failure should not depend on your address,
- the restrictive and content-laden nature of the curriculum,
- that examinations dominate teaching and encourage rote learning and uniformity rather than originality and imagination – they also put considerable pressure on learners, ("*At the moment we seem to be working merely for the sake of examinations, whereas we should work to satisfy our curiosities*", Patricia 15).

Particularly worrying was the consistent criticism of teachers as sometimes insulting, rude and cruel but more often as aloof, impatient, unable to recognise the simple importance of happiness in school, and their lack of enthusiasm. Teachers, the pupil respondents claim, have little time for the opinions of their pupils. They brush such opinions aside, ignore them or simply never elicit them.

Blishen identifies a key problem as teacher education itself which treats student teachers in an immature way and, by its own practices helps to produce inflexible teachers – "*there is a vicious circle, from school to college back to school, which goes on repeating a poor and unhelpful pattern of human relationships*". Teacher education, according to Blishen, perpetuates this vicious circle because *"often in their training, often too in the atmosphere of the system they enter, teachers are encouraged to think of their relationship with their children in limited terms...The nature of most of the teaching, thought of as a transfer of a set body of knowledge from teacher to child rather than as a creative contact open to surprise, easily sets a limit to the teacher's role. Because such teaching leads so often to boredom and frustration, the children (with all that is liveliest in them, their curiosity and half-grown opinions as well as their sense of fun, shut out of the classroom) fidget and fool, whereupon the teacher sets even fiercer, frostier limits to the relationship".*

From the responses of the pupils, Blishen identifies the characteristics or qualities of the new type of teacher that they would like to see: understanding, patient, encouraging, listening (to pupils), providing a chance for pupils to speak, humble, kind, capable of informality and simply pleasant. Teachers should establish links with parents, should be punctual, enthusiastic within reason, should not desert a school lightly, should recognise the importance to a child of being allowed to take the initiative in school work and, above all, be warm and personal. However, he comments that:

"It's quite difficult to be all these things with the present pattern of schooling, with the enclosed classrooms, the enclosed curriculum, under pressure from examinations...it really is very difficult to be the teacher children desire without enormous changes in the whole system. But any link in a vicious circle has some power to break the circle, and teachers can hardly fall back on a plea of impotence".

And, as an incentive to change, the respondents saw teachers both as enormously important to them and underpaid.

Blishen's final section in the book is simply called *Despotism Must Die*. He notes that discipline cannot really be separated from every other aspect of schooling as *"...a bored and unhappy creature has to be kept in a cage"*. What the children wanted was not disorder but a removal of irrelevant and petty rules, such as taking hands out of pockets. However,

"there is no argument about rules. The teachers know what is best. But responsible people are not created by imposing rules of conduct upon them, without discussion. Any rule that is not freely accepted, after debate, is likely to breed sullenness, furtive evasion. The children carry their argument very deep when they make, as many of them do, two particular points. The first is that anyone brought up for years under a regime that relies on an undiscussed network of rules is likely to lack self-discipline for themselves. The second point is that children of secondary age are, at their best, rebellious creatures. It is the quality of the young, for which we should be properly grateful, that they scrutinize the world around them with fresh eyes and are intensely critical of what they see. Human advance depends on this new, rash discontent. It needs not frustrating with arbitrary rules but schooling in the discussion of the bases of reasonable conduct. That critical energy needs to be enlisted, not alienated".

He comments that the title of the section *Despotism Must Die* may seem almost melodramatic but he asks the reader to read what the children have to say and see whether it has an trace of exaggeration in it. Here are some examples so that you can judge for yourself:

"I think it would be a very good idea to have less corporal punishment – as some of the methods these days are appalling, for instance, when a teacher hits you with the strap it makes you mutter at them and it also makes you despise them all the more" (Frances, 12).

"*All our teachers are allowed to belt and do so frequently. This makes boys have competitions to see who can get belted more often*" (Jane,14).

"*The discipline and life of the school would be based on freedom of the pupil. No uniforms and a minimum of control would be vital, and the pupils, male and female, would be treated as adults and allowed to see if they can live together in a community like intelligent people. Given this responsibility and freedom, the pupils would not obviously always be well-behaved and sensible, but they would, I believe, grow up mature and intelligent adults who are socially, and in all other respects, a benefit to the community*" (Christopher,16).

"*In this school the 'Big Powerful Headmaster' has no place, for no longer is he able to dismiss head boys, head girls and prefects, off his own bat; he has to consult the students' representatives. Neither he nor any member of his staff is able to deal out his or her version of justice without the victim having the right to appeal to a body consisting of both students and members of staff. This sort of doctrine may seem misguided to fervent upholders of tradition, but I ask them – think! Is it any more than each adult has come to regard as their undeniable right? The principle must be freedom from a tyranny of the headmaster is applicable to all schools. Despotism in education must die*" (Stephen,17).

Chapter two

Pedagogy of the Oppressed
by Paulo Freire
(Harmonsworth: Penguin, 1970)

Freire was a Brazilian writer and adult educator who was both imprisoned and exiled by the military regime in the 1960s. Freire's thinking about education, however, has implications for learning and teaching at all levels. Much of Freire's book is concerned with a theory of revolution and particularly with the need to avoid the danger of a revolution simply replacing one set of authoritarian oppressors and one dominant orthodoxy with a new one, albeit couched in revolutionary language. For present purposes the aim is to summarise the key points in Freire's analysis of the nature and potential of education itself.

Freire begins his book by arguing that the world is marked by dehumanisation, that is many people are thwarted by injustice, exploitation, oppression, alienation and violence of the oppressors, though many yearn to recover their lost humanity by overcoming oppression. However, it is crucial that the oppressed

"...*must not, in seeking to regain their humanity...become in turn the oppressors of the oppressors, but rather restorers of the humanity of both*".

i.e. that one orthodoxy does not simply replace another. This is a danger because the way of thinking of the oppressed has been conditioned by their experience and prescribed roles of oppression and this is now their model of humanity. This does not necessarily mean that the oppressed are unaware of being downtrodden but that their liberation is seen in terms of replacing the oppressor rather than a genuinely new alternative. The oppressed often fear freedom since it means replacing the security of the known with autonomy and responsibility.

In order to overcome oppression and realise a fuller sense of consciousness, it is important for people to critically recognise their oppression, its causes and the possibilities for transformation both of themselves and the world around them. This can only take place through a pedagogy of the oppressed based on critical dialogue and with a proclivity to action which is forged with, and not for, the learners, recognising that the teacher is also a learner and that the learner knows many things that the teacher does not know. Freire recognises that all education is inherently political and that any education offered as part of the existing system in an oppressive state and society will simply reproduce the ideas and interests of the oppressors. So, he prefers educational projects working with the oppressed to systemic education which can only be changed by political power. However, in such projects reflective participation (rather than monologues, slogans and communiqués) is crucial:

"A revolutionary leadership must accordingly practice **co-intentional** *education. Teachers and students (leadership and people), co-intent on reality, are both subjects, not only in the task of unveiling that reality, and thereby coming to know it critically, but in the task of re-creating that knowledge. As they attain this knowledge of reality through common reflection and action, they discover themselves as its permanent re-creators. In this way, the presence of the oppressed in the struggle for their liberation will be what it should be: not pseudo-participation, but committed involvement".*

Freire regards the usual teacher-student relationships as having a narrative character – the teacher speaks and the objects (students) listen so that **'Education is suffering from narration sickness'**:

"The teacher talks about reality as if it were motionless, static, compartmentalised and predictable...Their task is to 'fill' the students with the contents of his narration – contents which are detached from reality...Words that are emptied of their concreteness and become a hollow, alienated and alienating verbosity".

So, the abstract subject matter in education is often irrelevant to the learner who memorises it for no apparent reason, turning the learner into containers or receptacles to be filled by the teacher so that

"the more completely she fills the receptacles, the better a teacher she is. The more meekly the receptacles permit themselves to be filled, the better students they are".

Education of this type is therefore an act of 'depositing' and Freire refers to it as the 'banking' concept of education. But

"knowledge emerges only through invention and re-invention, through the restless, impatient, continuing, hopeful enquiry human beings pursue in the world, with the world, and with each other".

He summarises the oppressive nature of banking education as follows:

(a) the teacher teaches and the students are taught,
(b) the teacher knows everything and the students know nothing,
(c) the teacher thinks and the students are thought about,
(d) the teacher talks and the students listen – meekly,
(e) the teacher disciplines and the students are disciplined,
(f) the teacher chooses and enforces his choice, and the students comply,

(g) the teacher acts and the students give the illusion of acting through the action of the teacher,

(h) the teacher chooses the programme content, and the students (who were not consulted) adapt to it,

(i) the teacher confuses the authority of knowledge with his or her own professional authority, which he and she set in opposition to the freedom of the students,

(j) the teacher is the Subject of the learning process, while the pupils are mere Objects.

So that the more students work away at storing the deposited knowledge, the less they develop critical consciousness about the world around them and the more they accept their place in society and adapt to the world as it is, thereby posing little threat to the established, oppressive order. In this way it attempts to control thinking and action. He further describes this as **'Education as the exercise of domination'**.

This needs to be replaced by problem-posing education where issues are approached through dialogue, reflection and mutual learning. Teachers and students become jointly responsible for a process in which they all grow,

"whereas banking education anesthetises and inhibits creative power, problem-posing education involves a constant unveiling of reality. The former attempts to maintain the submersion of consciousness; the latter strives for the emergence of consciousness and critical intervention in reality".

This he regards as **'Education as the practice of freedom'.** In problem-posing education, people begin to perceive critically the way they exist in the world, not as a static reality but in a process of transformation. He further contrasts banking education with problem-posing education:

- Banking education attempts to conceal certain facts which explain the way human beings exist in the world whereas problem-posing education sets itself the task of demythologizing.
- Banking education resists dialogue whereas problem-posing education regards dialogue as an indispensable part of unveiling reality.
- Banking education treats students as objects of assistance whereas problem-posing education makes them critical thinkers.
- Banking education inhibits creativity and domesticates through controlling consciousness whereas problem-posing education stimulates true reflection and action upon reality.
- Banking education emphasises permanence and becomes reactionary whereas problem-posing education is rooted in the dynamic and changing present without a predetermined future.
- Banking education reinforces a fatalistic view of the world whereas a problem-posing education uses this very situation as a problem itself.

"*Problem-posing education does not and cannot serve the interests of the oppressor. No oppressive order could permit the oppressed to begin to question: Why?*"

For Freire, genuine dialogue involving critical thinking must take place in an atmosphere of humility, trust, hope and cooperation and be rooted in the historical and concrete reality of the participants. The themes that will be co-investigated as a result of dialogue will be therefore meaningful and significant to the learners. As an adult educator, literacy and language are important to Freire but they are not a technical exercise but rather an intensely political one because language shapes our understanding of the world, either reinforcing dominance and oppression or beginning to liberate people from oppression. A pedagogy of the oppressed involves decoding the meanings of language as used in a wide range of media and the purposes for which it is used. Hence the importance of people 'naming' i.e. unveiling the world in order to transform it through critical analysis of reality.

Chapter three

Compulsory Mis-Education
by Paul Goodman
(New York:Vintage Books, 1962)

Goodman begins his book with a longer version of the quote from Einstein that opens the book by Carl Rogers discussed below. Goodman also includes this bit:

"One had to cram all this stuff into one's mind, whether one liked it or not. This coercion had such a deterring effect that, after I had passed the final examination, I found the consideration of any scientific problems distasteful to me for an entire year".

In the preface Goodman notes that the dominance of the schooling as a 'given' prevents any new thinking about education, even though we are in unprecedented conditions. He asks whether we really need to perpetually expand access to the type of formal education presently provided or whether the faith in schools is part of a mass superstition. So that when there is, for example, a conference of experts on school drop-outs it is considered axiomatic that they ought to be in school (despite the fact that many drop out again soon after they have been cajoled back in). Yet,

"curiously muffled in these conferences is the question that puts the burden of proof the other way: What are they drop-outs from? Is the schooling really good for them, or much good for anybody? Since, for many, there are such difficulties with the present arrangements, might not some better arrangements be invented? Or bluntly, since schooling undertakes to be compulsory, must it not continually review its claim to be useful? Is it the only means of education?"

He asks, to what extent does the schooling system go on for its own sake, keeping more than a million people busy and providing a gigantic market for textbook manufacturers, building contractors and graduate Schools of Education. One other reason that the school system continues is that it plays an important role as a large and expensive baby-sitting service, given that in many families both parents go to work and in others there is only a single parent. Another is that it helps to keep the unemployed off the streets by 'putting them into concentration camps called schools'. Also, there is their valuable role as an arm of the police, providing cops and concentration camps paid for in the budget under the heading 'Board of Education'.

Different types of young people react differently to being made to attend this compulsory institution. Some, from middle class backgrounds, go through without complaining because of the prizes that lie ahead; others from very poor backgrounds might welcome the food and order that is on offer; others still conform and survive but drop out internally and day dream; while

"other poor youth, herded into a situation that does not fit their disposition, for which they are unprepared by their background, and which does not interest them, simply develop a reactive stupidity very different from their behaviour on the street or the ball field. They fall behind, play truant, and as soon as possible drop out. If the school situation is immediately useless and damaging to them, their response must be said to be life-preservative. They thereby somewhat diminish their chances of a decent living, but we shall see that the usual propaganda – that schooling is a road to high salaries is for most poor youth a lie; and the increase in security is arguably not worth the torture involved".

Early on in the book he suggests some alternatives to what he terms 'the system as a compulsory trap':

1. Have no school at all for a few classes as an experiment to see if it makes any difference. This can't do the children any academic harm since there is good evidence that normal children will make up the first seven years of school work with four to seven months of good teaching.

2. Dispense with school buildings for a few, small classes of about ten pupils - use the city itself as a school, its streets, cafeterias, stores, movies, museums, parks and factories. Where feasible, this makes more sense as it uses real subject-matter rather than an abstraction of subject-matter brought into the school building as 'curriculum'.

3. Both inside and outside the school building use appropriate unlicensed adults of the community – the druggist, storekeeper or mechanic – as proper educators of the young in a grown-up world. This helps to break down barriers and diminishes the 'omnivorous authority of professional school-people'.

4. Make class attendance not compulsory, in the manner of A.S.Neill's Summerhill – 'if the teachers are good, absence would tend to be eliminated; if they are bad, let them know it'.

5. Decentralise an urban school (or do not build a big new building) into small units of 20 to 50 of people of different grades or ages.

6. Use part of the school money to send children to economically marginal farms for a couple of months of the year to experience rural culture.

However, it may need to go further as schooling is no longer designed for the maximum growth and utility of children in a changing world and,

"*even when it is benevolent, it is in the bureaucratic death-grip of a uniformity of conception, from the universities down, that cannot possibly suit the multitude of dispositions and conditions...Thus, if we are going to experiment with real universal education that educates, we have to start by getting rid of compulsory schooling altogether".*

In a nutshell:

"At present, in most states, for 10 to 13 years, every young person is obliged to sit the better part of their day in a room which is almost always too crowded, facing front, doing lessons predetermined by a distant administration at the state capital and that has no relation to their own intellectual, social or animal interests, and not much relation even to their economic interests. The overcrowding precludes individuality or spontaneity, reduces the young to ciphers, and the teacher to a martinet. If a youth tries to follow their own bent, they are interrupted and even jailed. If they do not perform, they are humiliated and threatened but they are not allowed to fail and get out...Because of school work (young people) cannot follow their nose in reading and browsing in the library, or concentrate on a hobby that fires them, nor get a job, or carry on a responsible love affair or travel, or become involved in political action. The school system as a whole, with its increasingly set curriculum, stricter grading, incredible amounts of testing, is already a vast machine to shape acceptable responses".

Moreover, Goodman argues that schooling is often a form of brainwashing where a uniform world-view is presented without consideration of viable alternatives, there is confusion about the validity of one's own experience and feelings and a chronic anxiety so that pupils hang on to the uniform world view as security. This is because the 'social machine' does not necessarily want independence of mind, curiosity and initiative but orthodoxy, consensus and conformity. Yet, ironically, after all this conditioning young people are supposed to suddenly exercise initiative, find jobs for themselves, make career plans, undertake original artistic and scientific projects, marry, become parents and vote for public officers.

In order to improve matters so that schooling becomes even tolerable class sizes would have to be halved but this would require doubling budgets which he considers not to be a good idea as the money would be better spent in other ways. Essentially, education must become voluntary rather than compulsory as 'no growth to freedom occurs except by intrinsic motivation'. The present monolithic school system must give way to a much more diverse range of possibilities. He suggests giving school money to high-school-aged adolescents for any plausible self-chosen educational proposals such as purposeful travel or individual enterprise. This would also lead to the proliferation of experimental schools.

This kind of freedom, he argues, would be more in line with the American constitution and the educated and skilled electorate required of a democracy rather than the behaviour modification and programmed learning of much of schooling.

Goodman does not let higher education off lightly either:

"Disappointingly, but not surprisingly, the colleges and universities go along with this spiritual destruction, and indeed devise the tests and curricula to pass the tests..I do not expect for a moment that they will, in the foreseeable future, recall their primary duties: to pass on the tradition of disinterested learning, to provide a critical standard, to educate the free young to be free citizens and independent professionals".

Classes are not necessarily liberating but are a cash-accounting exercise of hours, tests, grades and credits with professors preoccupied by their own research.

He points out that at no other time or place in history have people believed that continuous schooling was the obvious means to prepare most youth for careers. While most careers required study, *"...it was never thought useful to give academic teaching in such massive and continuous doses as the only regimen"*. He suggests it would be a useful study to find out how many people who grew up from 1900 to 1920 and made great names in the sciences, arts, literature, government, business etc. actually went through the continuous sixteen year school grind without quitting, or without quitting and occasionally returning when it was relevant. The unfortunate part of the massive expansion of schooling was that,

"...insensibly, everybody began to believe that being in school was the only way to become an educated person. What a generation before had been the usual course, to quit school and seek elsewhere to grow up, became a sign of eccentricity, failure, delinquency".

He ends by enunciating the key principles on which he thinks education should be reformed:

- Make it easier for youngsters to gravitate to what suits them.
- Provide many points of quitting and return.
- Cut down on the loss of student hours in parroting and forgetting and the loss of teacher hours in talking to the deaf.
- Engage more directly in the work of society and have useful products to show instead of stacks of examination papers.

While he is pessimistic about the possibilities for change:

"Nevertheless, in my opinion, the present system is not viable; it is leading straight to 1984, which is not

viable. The change, when it comes, will not be practical and orderly".

Chapter four

The Betrayal of Youth
by James Hemming
(London: Marion Boyars, 1980)

The sub-title of this book is *Secondary Education must be Changed* and is based on British education, even though the points made may well be applicable elsewhere.

Hemming argues that the secondary education system is not serving the needs of adolescents well. At one extreme, among the academically successful, it can produce pressure and stress leading to psychological problems and sometimes a retreat into drugs and alcohol, while at the other,

"...the defeated rejects of the system sit out their schooldays in moods ranging from bored apathy to open hostility and leave school with their confidence and curiosity shattered, their powers of concentration atrophied, and a bitter hatred in their hearts for the society which has put them down".

He acknowledges that, of course, not all students become over-stressed and that some thrive on what school has to offer while others at least enjoy the friends they make at school. But even success at school or being happy there does not necessarily ensure the full development of the potential, capabilities and competence of young people:

*"Some schools achieve miracles, become havens of happy relationships and fulfilled growth to which students go willingly and which they leave as well-balanced individuals, with their self-esteem intact, prepared to tackle the challenges of adult life. But education of this type – the sort that **every***

adolescent has the right to expect – is attained in spite of the system rather than because of it. The weakness of the system is that it is not sufficiently concerned about individual development. It is too much tied up with routines of teaching and testing, accepting and rejecting. Consequently it has proved highly resistant to making the necessary fundamental changes".

A major part of the problem, Hemming argues, is that secondary education is not a mileu in which adolescents can flourish because it is not designed to suit them in the first place. Rather,

"...they have to fit as best they may into a framework of activities and demands which is imposed by habits of the past, and by authorities over which they have no control".

So, while adolescents can, of course, be cussed, their cussedness is usually provoked.

Hemming makes the simple point that you cannot expect adolescents to fully engage with an education that does not encourage or permit such engagement:

"What you cannot possibly do is to run the world of the classroom as an authoritarian system in which the pupils have no significant role except to submit, and, at the same time bring the energies of the students to a focus in the service of their own education... There is no more disheartening or undignified human employment than that of the teacher who feels obliged to try to teach material that young people can see no point in learning and who become more and more unmanageable as the attempt proceeds".

Hemming is also critical of the overwhelming focus on academic learning of subjects based on knowledge and concepts in secondary education which are squeezed into forty minute chunks. This distorts the educational process because it neglects other important attributes of human beings such as the intelligence of feeling, aesthetic awareness, imagination, intuition, judgement, breadth of apprehension, initiative, creative capacity, relational skill, manual proficiency and capability in general affairs.

Universities play a key role in this by assessing entrants primarily by their A level scores. He notes the contradiction of asking a candidate at interview 'What kind of person are you?' when the universities themselves are part of an educational system that imposes a narrow curriculum and lots of homework and which curtails time for private reading and personal development and adds:

"What is wrong is that academic values and competitiveness have run wild in education and that many in the education industry have a vested interest in keeping it that way"...whereas *"The educational system of a democracy should be just, humane, efficient and, above all, concerned with individual development – the nourishment of personal potential".*

Concomitant with this is the school's sole concern with the left hemisphere of the brain which specialises in linguistic, logical, abstract, convergent and sequential functions and the neglect of the right side of the brain which handles intuitional, synthetic, creative, relational, divergent and spatial functions. The net result is that school students are being educated lopsidedly and that school knowledge is seen as a hierarchy with music, drama, social studies seen as lightweights compared with the solid worth and maths and physics. So the significant innovators in education – Neill of Summerhill, Curry of Dartington, Badley of Bedales, John Dewey, Jerome Bruner and others sensed that something was wrong and tried to move education from the narrow to the broad, from excluding feeling to including it, from passive receptivity to active participation, from direction to spontaneity, from copying to creating, from the impersonal to the relational , from the academic to the human and from the isolated to the social. Schools, he argues, need a balance between the right and left attributes of the brain if they are going to serve all children well.

So what are the basic elements of human competence that schools should educate for? In terms of personal competence he lists the ability to:

- Communicate thoughts and feelings by speech and writing.
- Handle numbers, money and mensuration in real-life situations.
- Evaluate statistical statements on everyday issues and to understand the meaning of probability and 'average'.
- Read fluently.
- Earn one's own living.
- Entertain oneself.
- Relate to others.
- Accept responsibility for oneself.
- Be sensitive to the needs and feelings of others.
- Be able to think laterally as well as linearly.
- Listen to what others are saying.
- Reason with intelligence and feeling.

In terms of social competence he lists the ability to:

- Make intelligent choices between alternatives.
- Cooperate with others in the pursuit of common aims..
- Take the initiative when it is appropriate to do so.
- Set oneself realistic goals.
- Tackle complex situations.
- Understand and accept emotions.
- Tolerate unavoidable frustrations.
- Acquire a set of principles by which to live.

Overall, his desirable personal qualities are self-reliance, confidence, curiosity, concentration, persistence, reliability, flexibility, far-sightedness and imagination. Hemming cites research carried out in Britain in the late 1970s showing that many teachers felt that educating for such qualities was important but that, due to the examination system, significantly smaller percentages actually tried hard to achieve the aim and only minorities felt that they were moderately successful in achieving the aim. He also notes that only 13% of the teachers thought that 'Encourage them to have a good time' was an important aim of education and quotes Pestalozzi to the effect that 'No subject is worth a sou if it destroys courage and joy'.

And, for Hemming, this is the problem with Britain's schooling as there is a profound motivation crisis with both pupils who are less able academically and those who are highly capable being bored or feeling that school has little to offer them. As he notes, thousands of adolescents vote with their feet every day and stay away from school on one pretext or another. He cites evidence from the time as to lack of enthusiasm about going to school, which is more pronounced among those heading for manual occupations than middle class ones. This situation also has a negative affect on many teachers, though it varies:

"Teachers, from their side, are often numb, shaken and humiliated by the blatant disregard for what they have on offer. Some leave the profession in despair; some armour themselves with cynicism; and some struggle on in a condition of depressed malaise. Others ride the storms and stay with the kids, physically and in spirit, in all kinds of difficult circumstances. Then there are those, yet again, who find themselves in pleasant schools and sail happily before the wind, rarely running into bad weather".

What is required in schools is more emphasis on personalised education to meet the needs and aims of learners, rather than teachers, schools, education systems or governments. The main priority for schooling must be to humanise through a community built on friendliness, cooperation and democracy rather than an autocratic one in which the subordinate members are left with no choice but to conform or rebel. A more democratic form of schooling, while right in itself as a form of preparation for democracy in the wider society, also has benefits for the school:

"Most people – including adolescents – will behave reasonably if the circumstances are reasonable. In contrast, where there is a staff-versus-pupil atmosphere in a school, there is no incentive for the pupils to guide their own or others' behaviour; the cooperative principle is simply not to be found…adolescents who are treated like children will behave like children. It is within the framework of a democratic school community that opportunities readily arise for those relationships and encounters which promote the development of personal competence".

Congruent with this is that everybody is treated with dignity, which is also why corporal punishment has no place in school. Assessment is also an important consideration as

"it can only be justified within the process of education if it does not damage young people and if it is accurate and fair. The means commonly in use in Great Britain today, though not only in Britain, meet none of these criteria".

Hemming then casts doubt on the objectivity of examination systems both in schools and universities and suggests instead that there should be an educational system in which the growth and purposes of students are central and where students can use exams or assignments to test themselves against their own previous achievements in cooperation with teachers. *"You cannot have, at one and the same time, education for personal growth and a totally impersonal system of assessment".* To him some form of student profiling seems *"...the most humane and least deleterious way of evaluating personality and attainments for university and job selection".*

The final chapter of the book ends by looking to the future and, considering it was written in 1978/9, contains a shockingly accurate prediction of the world-wide web and the internet:

"For a fee, we shall be linked up to the world memory bank – a vast electronic extension of the individual human brain".

But mostly he stresses the importance of changing education to avoid catastrophe 'in the form of a kid-glove 1984' where control is exercised over the masses through manipulation and a diet of bread and circuses. The only antidote is a fully educated citizenry produced by an education system based on the sort of values and practices that Hemming describes, but that requires significant change.

Chapter five

How Children Fail
by John Holt
(Harmondsworth: Penguin, 1969)

"You know, kids really like to learn; we just don't like being pushed around."

John Holt's book, originally published in 1964, is essentially the work of a reflective practitioner. It takes the form of a series of memos between 1958 and 1960 in which he interrogates his practice as a maths teacher in a primary school and considers the wider implications for education. This in itself is interesting in the light of those who claim that 'politics should be kept out of education'. Holt starts with what some might think a fairly 'factual' subject but as soon as any form of knowledge is put into an educational setting the ensuing human relationships ensure that much wider issues arise. Not only is he acutely aware of the political nature of education (*'Even in the most non-controversial areas of our teaching, the books and the textbooks we give children present a dishonest and distorted picture of the world'*) but for Holt, the issues that arise cause deep concern about the nature of schooling.

Holt's main conclusion is that, whereas children begin life with an extraordinary capacity and enthusiasm for learning, schooling does its best to destroy this by the things schools do to them and make them do:

"We destroy this capacity above all by making them afraid, afraid of not doing what other people want, of not pleasing, of making mistakes, of failing, of being wrong...we like children who are a little afraid of us, docile, deferential children".

This is achieved partly by the intensely competitive nature of schooling replete with grades, gold stars, examinations, tests, rankings and prizes but also by boring them,

"...by filling up their days with dull, repetitive tasks that make little or no claim on their attention or demands on their intelligence. Our hearts leap with joy at the sight of a roomful of children all slogging away at some imposed task and we are all the more pleased and satisfied if someone tells us that children really don't like what they are doing. We tell ourselves that this drudgery, this endless busywork, is good preparation for life and we fear that without it children would be hard to 'control'...By such means children are firmly established in the habit of using only a small part of their thinking capacity. They feel that school is a place where they must spend most of their time doing dull tasks in a dull way".

Parents, he notes, can be complicit in this, some having urged him to crack down on their children:

"Do such people see school as an institutionalised punishment, something unpleasant that we can do to children whether or not they have done anything to deserve it? What is it that such people resent about children?"

There is also far too much emphasis on 'right answerism' in schools – about guessing what the teacher or the exam regards as the right answer rather than processes of learning and a spirit of enquiry. Moreover, much of school-based knowledge learning is quickly forgotten and is not of much use or interest in the first place. Indeed, Holt regards the notion of a curriculum as an essential body of knowledge as absurd. Even if children did remember it, not only can adults not agree on what knowledge is essential but the rapid changes in knowledge meant that what is learnt as 'true' can soon be redundant and revised. How can we possibly predict what knowledge will be most needed ten, twenty or forty years from now?

He asks the ever more pertinent question, are we trying to turn out intelligent people and develop human qualities or produce test-takers? As regards the quest for intelligent people,

"...we'll never do it as long as we are obsessed with tests. At faculty meetings we talk about how to reward the thinkers in our classes. Who is kidding whom? No amount of rewards and satisfactions obtained in the small group thinking sessions will make up to Monica for what she felt today, faced by a final test that she knew she couldn't do and was going to fail. Pleasant experiences don't make up for painful ones. No child, once painfully burned, would agree to be burned again, however enticing the reward. For all our talk and good intentions, there is much more stick that carrot in school..."

The constant testing and cramming because of the fetish with high test scores which they call high standards leads young people to conclude that "school is mainly a place where you follow meaningless procedures to get meaningless answers to meaningless questions".

Behind the competitive knowledge-cramming is a system that exists to fail cohorts at various stages, to prepare for a stratified workforce and society. Fear of failure is therefore ever present: "It is no coincidence that in many of their worst nightmares adults find themselves back in school". He points out that when a baby makes mistakes he or she just tries again because they have not learnt that not getting right first time is a cause of shame and disgrace. For a baby, learning is a cause of satisfaction in itself, whether or not anybody else notices. Revealingly, in the light of contemporary complaints about various groups of young people 'underachieving' or being hostile in school, he notes that many children may calculate that if they cannot have the rare commodity of total success, the next best option might well be total failure as a way of avoiding pressure and irrelevant and unrealistic expectations. And they give adults a hard time because adults have given them a hard time.

So why do children go to school if it is so boring, irrelevant and unpleasant much of the time? Because they have to. Holt ruefully comes to the conclusion that,

"...the valiant and resolute band of travellers I thought I was leading towards a much-hoped for destination turned out instead to be more like convicts in a chain gang, forced under threat of punishment to move along a rough path leading nobody knew where, and down which they could see hardly more that a few steps ahead. School feels like this to children: it is a place where they make you go and where they tell you to do things and where they try to make your life unpleasant if you don't do them or don't do them right".

As a result children either avoid the tasks altogether or get them done with a minimum of effort and unpleasantness. But the net result is that for many children school is a kind of jail where they deliberately *go stupid* to deny their intelligence to the jailers as a form of resistance:

"Freedom to live and think about life for its own sake is important and even essential to a child. They will only give so much time and thought to what others want them to do; the rest they demand and take for their own interests, plans, worries, dreams. The result is that they are not all there during most hours of school...fear, boredom, resistance – they all go to make what we call stupid children".

The hypocrisy of all this is that we ask children to do for most of the day what few adults are even able to do for an hour:

"*How many of us, attending, say, a lecture that doesn't interest us, can keep our minds from wandering? Hardly any. Not I certainly. Yet children have far less awareness of and control of their attentions than we do...The case against boredom in school is that it makes children stupid, some on purpose, most because they cannot help it*".

This of course raises the question of why we do things in schools the way we do. Is the real purpose of schooling the learning of children or control by adults?

"*Do we do something because we want to help the children and can see that what we are doing is helping them? Or do we do it because it is inexpensive or convenient for school, teachers, adminstrators? Or because everyone else is doing it?*"

Instead of coercion, boredom and one size fits all:

"*Schools should be a place where children learn what they most want to know, instead of what we think they ought to know...schools and classrooms in which each child in their own way can satisfy their curiosity, develop their abilities and talents, pursue their interests, and from the adults and other children around them, get a glimpse of the great variety and richness of life. In short, the school should be helping them? Or do we do it because it is a smorgasbord of intellectual, artistic, creative and athletic activities, from which each child could take whatever they wanted, and as much as they wanted, or as little*".

Chapter six

Dechooling Society
by Ivan Illich
(Marion Boyars: London, 1971)

"...for most people the right to learn is curtailed by the obligation to attend school."

"Adults tend to romanticise their schooling...But the same adults would worry about the mental health of a child who rushed home to tell them what they had learned from every teacher."

Illich makes the case that education has become institutionalised in schools and schools are therefore mistaken for education. This has created a reliance on, and automatic belief in, schools as the only source of education and a perceived need to spend ever more money on schooling:

"School has become the world religion of a modernised proletariat, and makes futile promises of salvation to the poor of the technological age. The nation-state has adopted it, drafting all citizens into a graded curriculum leading to sequential diplomas not unlike the initiation rituals and hieratic promotions of former times. The modern state has assumed the duty of enforcing the judgement of its educators through well-meant truant officers and job requirements, much as did the Spanish kings who enforced the judgements of their theologians through the conquistadors and the Inquisition".

But schooling is not necessarily the same thing as education:

"The pupil is thereby 'schooled' to confuse teaching with learning, grade advancement with education, a

diploma with competence and fluency with the ability to say something new".

Schooling is a costly, self-perpetuating institution that creates its own demands for more of the same, yet no society, least of all developing societies, can ever genuinely meet the full cost of schooling for all. But the school monopoly of official education is also harmful because it renders individual accomplishment suspect, prevents people from taking control of their own learning and does not serve personal, creative and autonomous interaction.

Despite rhetoric to the contrary, schooling also contributes to the reproduction of social inequality:

"It should be obvious that even with schools of equal quality a poor child can seldom catch up with a rich one. Even if they attend schools and begin at the same age, poor children lack most of the educational opportunities which are casually available to the middle-class child. These advantages range from conversation and books in the home to vacation travel and a different sense of oneself, and apply, for the child who enjoys them, both in and out of school. So the poorer student will generally fall behind so long as they depend on school for advancement or learning. The poor need funds to enable them to learn, not to get certified for the treatment of their alleged disproportionate deficiencies".

In those countries where some children go to school and some do not, the latter are schooled in a sense of inferiority toward the better-schooled:

"Their fanaticism in favour of school makes it possible to exploit them doubly: it permits increasing allocation of public funds for the education of a few and increasing acceptance of social control by the many".

Schooling also helps to reproduce inequality internationally by grading and ranking the nations of the world by how much schooling they provide as well as their per capita gross national product, creating an international caste system.

A major, mistaken, assumption of schooling is that most learning is the result of teaching, yet most learning happens casually outside school:

"Increasingly educational research demonstrates that children learn most of what teachers pretend to teach them from peer groups, from comics, from chance observations, and above all from mere participation in the ritual of the school. Teachers, more often than not, obstruct such learning of subject matters as goes on in school."

Most learning is not the result of instruction but rather the result of unhampered participation in a meaningful setting. Illich suggests separating the learning of basic skills from other aspects of education. He suggests free and competing skill centres where people can learn a whole range of basic skills such as language, numeracy, computing, plumbing driving, wiring, diving by drill training:

"The deschooling of society implies a recognition of the two-faced nature of learning. An insistence on skill drill alone could be a disaster; equal emphasis must be placed on other kinds of learning. But if schools are the wrong places for learning a skill, they are even worse places for getting an education. School does both tasks badly, partly because it does not distinguish between them. School is inefficient in skill instruction especially because it is curricular. In most schools a programme which is meant to improve one skill is chained always to another irrelevant task. History is tied to advancement in maths, and class attendance to the right to use the playground".

Whereas most skills can be acquired and improved by drills, education relies on the critical intent to use memories creatively. Education relies on the surprise of the unexpected question which opens new doors for enquirers. Creative exploratory learning, according to Illich, requires peers currently puzzled about the same terms or problems so that even though

"large universities make the futile attempt to match them by multiplying their courses, they generally fail since they are bound to curriculum, course structure and bureaucratic administration. In schools, including universities, most resources are spent to purchase the time and motivation of a limited number of people to take predetermined problems in a ritually defined setting".

The whole enterprise is by definition teacher-centred because it requires an authoritarian presence to define for the participants their starting point for discussion. The fundamental approach common to all schools is the idea that one person's judgement should determine what and when another person must learn. Indeed,

"the claim that a liberal society can be founded on the modern school is paradoxical. The safeguards of individual freedom are cancelled in the dealings of teachers with pupils. When the schoolteacher fuses in their person the functions of judge, ideologue and doctor, the fundamental style of society is perverted by the very process which should prepare for life".

He sees the latent functions of schooling as custodial care, selection, indoctrination and learning. He argues that the grouping of people by age in schools results from modern conceptions of the separation of the categories of childhood and adulthood, the only way that it is possible to get human beings to submit to the authority of the schoolteacher:

"Defining children as full-time pupils permits the teacher to exercise a kind of power over their persons which is much less limited by constitutional and consuetudinal restrictions than the power wielded by the guardians of other social enclaves. Their

chronological age disqualifies children from safeguards which are routine for adults in a modern asylum, madhouse, monastery or jail".

The school world is one where everything can be quantified and measured and what cannot be measured is of no value and threatening. It is also the world of the assembly line:

"The distributor-teacher delivers finished product to the consumer-pupil, whose reactions are carefully studied and charted to provide research data for the preparation of the next model, which may be 'ungraded', 'student-designed', 'team taught', 'visually-aided' or 'issue-centred' ".

In fact, by teaching the need to be taught, schooling provides a preparatory form of alienation for institutionalised life and work and,

"once this lesson is learned, people lose their incentive to grow in independence; they no longer find relatedness attractive and close themselves off to the surprises which life offers when it is not predetermined by institutional definition...only school is credited with the principal function of forming critical judgement, and, paradoxically, tries to do so by making learning about oneself, about others and about nature depend on a pre-packaged process".

He argues that learners should not be forced to submit to an obligatory curriculum and the public should not be forced to support, through regressive taxation, a huge professional apparatus of educators and buildings. Schools are designed on the assumption that there is a secret to everything in life, that the quality of life depends on knowing that secret, that secrets can only be known in orderly succession and that only teachers can properly reveal these secrets. He concludes that the institution of school needs to go, as he thinks it will in the near future, and be replaced by a system based on self-motivated learning,

"...instead of employing teachers to bribe or compel the student to find the time and the will to learn; that we can provide the learner with new links to the world instead of continuing to funnel all educational programmes through the teacher".

The goals which guide this educational revolution would be as follows:

1. To liberate access to things by abolishing the control which persons and institutions now exercise over their educational values.
2. To liberate the sharing of skills by guaranteeing freedom to teach or exercise them on request.
3. To liberate the critical and creative resources of people by returning to individual persons the ability to call and hold meetings – an ability now increasingly monopolised by institutions which claim to speak for the people.
4. To liberate individuals from the obligation to shape their expectations to the services offered by any established profession by providing them with the opportunity to draw on the experience of peers and entrust themselves to a teacher, guide, adviser or healer of choice.

He puts forward the idea of learning webs or networks. He uses four examples which enable the student to gain access to any educational resource that may help them to achieve their own goals:

1. Reference services to educational objects – which facilitate access to things or processes used for formal learning. Some of these can be reserved for this purpose, stored in libraries, rental agencies, laboratories and showrooms like museums and theatres and others can be

in daily use in factories, airports or on farms but made available to students as apprentices or on off-hours.

2. Skill exchanges – which permit persons to list their skills, the conditions under which they are willing to serve as models for others who want to learn these skills and the addresses at which they can be reached.

3. Peer-matching – a communication network which permits persons to describe the learning activity in which they wish to engage in the hope of finding a partner for the enquiry.

4. Reference services to educators-at-large – who can be listed in a directory giving the addresses and self-descriptions of professionals, paraprofessionals, and free-lancers, along with conditions of access to their services. Such educators could be chosen by polling or consulting their former clients.

Chapter seven

Life in Classrooms
by Philip W. Jackson
(New York: Holt, Rinehart and Winston, 1968)

This book differs from many of the others reviewed here in that it takes a more sociological approach to analysing the everyday, taken-for-granted detail of the routines of elementary or primary schooling. It does not start out with an existing critique of schooling but simply retains an open mind and discusses in a matter of fact way what can be observed and what survey evidence has revealed.

The first chapter is called *The Daily Grind* and the immediate factor that Jackson draws attention to is the compulsory nature of schooling:

"We must recognise, in other words, that children are in school for a long time, that the settings in which they perform are highly uniform and that they are there whether they want to be or not".

He comments further that,

"there is an important fact about a student's life that teachers and parents often prefer not to talk about, at least not in front of students. This is the fact that young people have to be in school whether they want to be or not. In this regard students have something in common with the members of two other of our social institutions that have involuntary attendance: prisons and mental hospitals. The analogy, though dramatic, is not intended to be shocking, and certainly there is no comparison between the unpleasantness of life for inmates in our prisons and mental institutions, on the one hand, and the daily travails of a first or second grader, on the other. Yet the school child, like the incarcerated adult, is, in a

sense, a prisoner. They too must come to grips with the inevitability of the experience. They too must develop strategies for dealing with the conflict that frequently arises between their natural desires and interests on the one hand and institutional expectations on the other".

And even within school, "...things happen not because students want them to, but because it is time for them to occur...Students are there whether they want to be or not and the work on which they are expected to concentrate also is often not of their own choosing".

The authority of the teacher is central and in reality differs very little between schools that appear more 'progressive' and those that appear more 'traditional':

"Even a first grader knows that an absent teacher requires a substitute whereas an absent student does not".

He compares the sheer duration of schooling to attending a church service, and notes that a child would have to attend a church service for a whole day for 24 years to equal the experience of school that a twelve-year-old already has.

Also of note are the crowded conditions:

"Even factory workers are not clustered as close together as students in a standard classroom. Indeed, imagine what would happen if a factory the size of a typical elementary school contained three or four hundred workers. In all likelihood the unions would not allow it".

Yet, despite this close proximity, students are expected to behave as though they were in solitude:

"They must keep their eyes on their paper when human faces beckon. Indeed, in the early grades it is *not uncommon to find students facing each other around a table while at the same time being required not to communicate with each other. These young people, if they are to become successful students, must learn how to be alone in a crowd".*

Early on students learn that rewards come from doing what the teacher says but compliance is not the only strategy of avoiding a difficult time. Another is by disguising the failure to comply – by cheating. The most high profile of these is of course cheating in tests, but students also misinform by putting their hand up when they do not know an answer or when the teacher enquires who in the class has done their homework. These students are cheating as much as those that fake interest during a classroom discussion:

"Each represents an effort to avoid censure or win unwarranted praise. Such efforts are far more common in the classroom than our focus on cheating in test situations would have us believe. Learning how to make it in school involves, in part, learning how to falsify behaviour"

All of this is not unconnected to socialisation for future roles in the labour force, the teacher being the student's first 'Boss' and

"...this skill in complying with educational authority is doubly important because the student will be called upon to put it to work in many out of school settings. The transition from classroom to factory or office is made easily by those who have developed 'good work habits' in their early years...So far as their power structure is concerned classrooms are not too dissimilar from factories or offices, those ubiquitous organisations in which so much of our adult life is spent".

Unfortunately, the daily routine of power structures in schools does not sit necessarily comfortably with critical thinking and with what Jackson terms 'scholarship', as

"the curious person typically engages in a kind of probing, poking, and exploring that is almost antithetical to the attitude of the passive conformist. The scholar must develop the habit of challenging authority and questioning the value of tradition".

Chapter eight

Education and Ecstasy
by George Leonard
(London: John Murray, 1970)

"School is a terrible thing to do to kids. It's cruel, unnatural and unnecessary...schools as they now exist are well-designed to produce unhappiness and little else."

Leonard began studying education by accident on a journalistic assignment. Sometimes an innocent approach and a fresh pair of eyes can make the familiar look very different and after twelve years he wrote this book. He begins the book by asking *'What is education?'* In terms of formal schooling in America, he is not impressed. The main task and purpose of schooling seems to be the conservative function of taming and controlling the pupils in order to prevent the new generation from changing in any deep or significant way. Fifty minutes of an hour in the classroom is taken up by control - the ubiquitous SHHH! from the teacher. If the teacher is lucky, then occasionally the class may be fully teachable and genuine moments of learning can take place, even in school, though this is far from common. However, learning is always taking place, even if it is negative learning:

"Some pupils learn how to daydream; others, how to take tests. Some learn the petty deceptions involved in cheating; others, the larger deceptions of playing the school game absolutely straight (the well-kept notebook, the right answer, the senior who majors in good grades). Most learn that the symbolic tricks their keepers attempt to teach them have little to do with their own deeper feelings or anything in the here and now. The activity that masquerades under the ancient

and noble aim of 'education' actually seems to serve as some sort of ransom to the future, a down payment on 'getting ahead' – or at least toward not falling behind".

He reminds us that school is a relatively recent social construct and until recently only a tiny proportion of the West's population saw the inside of a school. However, since their introduction,

"for the most part, the schools have not really changed...The most common mode of instruction today, as in the Renaissance, has a teacher sitting or standing before a number of students in a single room, presenting them with facts and techniques of a verbal-rational nature. Our expectations of what the human animal can learn, can do, can be, remains remarkably low and timorous. Our definition of education's root purpose remains short-sightedly utilitarian. Our map of the territory of learning remains antiquated".

Education has not necessarily made people happy on the whole or offered them ways to change deep down, so that 'A visitor from another planet might conclude that our schools are hell-bent on creating...a generation of joyless drudges'.

Society seems to sense that change is needed in the light of rapid social change and that education should play a role but nothing happens:

"We sense that salvation lies in education; so we trifle around the edges of things pedagogical and call it 'revolution'. When nothing much happens, we turn on the educators with a harshness that dishonours not them but ourselves. We damn them as mere baby-sitters when this is the function we most avidly press upon them...No, educators are not the culprits. They are the valiant slaves of our society, condemned to perpetuate the very system that victimises them".

Yet, ways can be worked out to change education to make learning more pleasurable, more relevant to learning for an uncertain future, a more cooperative and less adversarial task for teachers and learners and a lifelong pursuit for everyone. Education should be aimed at ecstasy or the ultimate delight of learning and discovery. But, for Leonard, to learn is to change.

What about the possibility of removing schools altogether?

"Presently everything that is being accomplished in the schools can be accomplished more effectively and with less pain in the average child's home and neighbourhood playground...you can find no evidence that the teacher per se helps learning. You can find much evidence that the teacher does harm to the learning process. The average school, in fact, is no fit place to learn in. It is basically a lock-up, a jail. Its most basic conditions create a resistance to learning. Physically, the child is worn down by the fatigue of sitting in one position for inordinate lengths of time. Mentally pupils are stunned by the sameness of their surroundings and the monotony of the stimuli that bombard them."

New teachers are told that classroom control and learning to take instructions must come first, and most 'learning' takes the form of giving the teacher back what the teacher wants to hear. Pupils learn to sit still, to take instructions, line up in orderly rows, to feel guilt for their natural impulses and perhaps to do a few simple things that they could learn to do in one fiftieth of the time it usually takes them. Indeed, he argues that with everything else that is going on in school, there is less that ten percent of any child's time left for anything that can be termed 'learning'.

Schools and colleges have served a society that needed reliable, predictable human components so capabilities that seemed at odds with this were not countenanced. Educational institutions were therefore geared to *stop* learning and replace it with right answers and an experience that was mostly dull, painful and based on the twin motivators of competition and punishment.

In answering the question, 'Schools – for what?', he suggests that education should have the following purposes:

- To learn the commonly agreed-upon skills and knowledge of the ongoing culture (reading, writing, figuring, history and the like), to learn it joyfully and to learn that all of it, even the most sacred 'fact', is strictly tentative.
- To learn how to ring creative changes on all that is currently agreed upon.
- To learn delight, not aggression; sharing, not eager acquisition; uniqueness, not narrow competition.
- To learn heightened awareness and control of emotional, sensory and bodily states and, through this, increased empathy for other people (a new kind of citizenship education).
- To learn how to enter and enjoy varying states of consciousness, in preparation for a life of change.
- To learn how to explore and enjoy the infinite possibilities in relations between people, perhaps the most common form of escstasy.
- To learn how to learn, for learning – one word that includes singing, dancing, interacting and much more – is already becoming the main purpose of life.

And, among other strategies for change such as publicising schools that already adopt such an approach, he also stresses the importance of the family which

"*...can become perhaps the most powerful agency of education and the reform of education. Parents have*

*the very first opportunity to create joyful and effective
learning environments for their children".*

Chapter nine

The Little Red School Book
by Soren Hansen and Jasper Jensen
(London: Stage 1, 1971)

The title of this little red book comes from the little red book of Mao Tse Tung fame and it starts with a neo-Marxist analysis of the education system:

"*The system is controlled by the people who have the money, and directly and indirectly these people decide what you should be taught and how. Whatever teachers and politicians may say, the aim of the education system in Britain is not to give you the best possible opportunity of developing your own talents. The industries and businesses that control our economic system need a relatively small number of highly educated experts to do the brain-work, and a large number of less educated people to do the donkey-work...Schools have to teach you to obey authority rather than to question things, just as the exam system encourages you to conform, not to be an individual. And teachers and others who are against this system can't do much about it on their own*".

Part of this is learning to do boring things because then pupils learn about duty and obeying orders later in life. However, the authors argue that this should not be the case because school should give each individual pupils as many learning opportunities as possible yet:

"*Remember that everything you've learnt you've learnt yourself. You have to do the work of learning. Your teacher can't do it for you...Remember that you can only learn about things if you're allowed to think them out for yourself...If you're forced to learn, you learn that learning is unpleasant. It's no help that the teachers says it will come in useful later in life. If you're not given any responsibility or allowed to choose or decide anything for yourself, you learn to be irresponsible and to depend on others, even if your work gets 10 out of 10".*

The book also contains useful tips about how to complain politely and work with teachers if lessons are boring and irrelevant, noting that if this does not work the result is usually that pupils muck about. The book, in fact, takes a very responsible and positive tone on this (and a lot of other issues):

"Never muck about unless you're absolutely certain that the teacher is an incurable bore and you've tried every way of persuading them to change. But remember – even if a teacher is a bore, mucking about won't actually solve the problem. You'll have to take more positive action".

The book argues that the most common type of teaching is some form of whole class teaching with the teacher firmly in control of content, noting that teachers who do give pupils a say in what they learn and how may face criticism from parents and colleagues.

The authors see teachers as playing a fairly conservative role but do not necessarily blame the individuals:

"Many teachers don't really question the true value of the things they teach you...These teachers often accept the world pretty much as it is. All this is not the teacher's fault. They work at school every day. They are forced to prepare you for exams set by other people with which they themselves may disagree".

The book suggests that teachers should get sabbaticals to get experience of something other than teaching. It also explains sympathetically about teachers' workload and low pay but also describes the kind of information a school possesses about pupils which is available to teachers, social workers, police and others. It also, realistically, notes that teachers do not always agree with each other and that

"many teachers are afraid of losing their job or not getting promoted. For this reason they don't dare speak out if they disagree with the head teacher or the head of department. So it's rare for a teacher to dare to tell pupils what they really think about the conditions at school…When it comes down to it teachers have remarkably little control over their lives – if they want to remain teachers that is".

The authors note that most schools operate as a hierarchy with pupils at the bottom, though it would be better if ideas could be exchanged freely in school and everyone could have a say based on mutual respect in a more democratic fashion. In the meantime the book contains a variety of practical tips about how to change things in school, from the school council and magazine to complaints, demonstrations and strikes – at all times emphasising the need to be polite and peaceful and to cooperate wherever possible.

The authors take particular issue with corporal punishment:

"Corporal punishment in schools is obsolete and should be abolished. It's been abolished in British prisons and the army and navy. It's been abolished in schools in most other Western countries. Why is it still used in most British schools?"

They also take issue with military training in schools such as the Combined Cadet Force, thereby reinforcing the idea that war is at least necessary, if not a good thing, and at the same time helping with recruitment to the armed forces.

There is also a strong plea for inclusivity – that all pupils are different and that all should treat each other with respect, noting that when there is talk of pupils with learning difficulties not coping at school what should be said is that school cannot cope with them. It also important to resist taken for granted convention for its own sake and to think for yourself:

"You are a person in your own right.
In the end you're accountable only to yourself for your own actions.
You don't have to play the part given you by your teachers and parents. You've got ideas of your own and usually know what you want.
You know something.
You don't know everything.
You're as good as anybody else.
You're not perfect.
You can learn something from others and others can learn from you".

After a lengthy excursion into sex and drugs education the book concludes with some interesting comments about the education system, given that "only a few schools are places that children and young people enjoy being in":

"Grown ups built your school and paid for it. They decide how things should be in the school. But it's you who use the school and first and foremost it's your place of work. Teachers work there too, of course, but if you weren't there, they wouldn't have a job and wouldn't get paid. Teachers don't have to work in schools. You do. School is the only place in Britain where everyone must spend ten years of their life...So if you want a better school the only thing you can do is to start changing the one you've already got".

It reserves a particularly strong criticism for the nature and role of exams:

"In some schools teachers believe that exams and tests show exactly what you know. By far the greatest number of exams don't show what you know. They often ask the wrong questions. They may show what you've learned parrot-fashion or had knocked into you. They rarely show whether you can think for yourself and find things out for yourself...You're not allowed to discuss the questions with your friends. You may be nervous or ill at the time. You don't get enough time to think about the questions and write the answers. So it's not people who know most who do best in exams; it's the people who are properly organised, can keep cool and can write fast" – in other words exams often get in the way of education.

And it is not very keen on school uniforms, unusual in other European countries, arguing that they do not in reality disguise differences in parental income and that there are better ways of making pupils feel more part of a school community. Interesting, for the time it was written, The Little Red School Book is also highly critical of unequal way the genders are treated in school.

The book ends with strong support for school councils as "Very few British schools have a school council, and very few of the ones that do exist have any real power", even though "a school council or similar body can be a very good way of learning how democracy works or doesn't work..." True to form the book provides practical advice about organising a school council and the nature of the culture of democracy needed to support it and make it work, noting that

"nearly all the changes in which you're allowed to participate are things which aren't very important. The real and difficult changes are those which give more and more people power to decide more and more things for themselves".

Chapter ten

Education for Self-Reliance
by Julius Nyerere
(Dar Es Salaam: Government Printer, 1967)

Julius Nyerere, a former teacher, was the first President of an independent Tanzania. He set Tanzania upon a path of what he termed 'African socialism' which would be based on the traditional communal values of African villages that had been destroyed by colonialism. Development would be based on cooperative agriculture in self-reliant communities in rural areas.

Nyerere saw education as the key to creating a new set of values. Nyerere argued that the scarcity of opportunities for education and the characteristics of teaching and learning strongly reinforced the prevalence of individualism and competition in the education system. Many pupils went to boarding schools which removed them from contact with their communities. As a result many were estranged from the problems of their society, wishing to obtain the privileges and comforts of salaried employment, and they increasingly adopted narrow and elitist attitudes. There was a danger that schools would become institutions of the reproduction of social inequality rather than engines of development for all.

Nyerere argued that schools therefore needed to be more closely integrated with the local community through productive enterprise. Each school would possess a farm or other productive enterprise and thus schooling would not be divorced from the agricultural production of the surrounding society.

He further argued that the pressure of examinations and syllabuses based on the memorisation of large amounts of knowledge had led to classrooms that were didactic and authoritarian in nature with teachers simply transmitting information to be learned by rote. Instead, the power should be moved from the teacher to the learner by placing more emphasis on active, participatory and cooperative classroom methods such as problem-solving and enquiry-based project work, and by adding character assessment to formal examinations. In the school as a whole, pupils should be given the opportunity to make many of the decisions about the school's productive enterprise and thus learn to value and practice participation and direct democracy. This would require school councils and more democratic forms of school organisation. Teacher training would need to be reformed so that teachers were trained for a new type of education system. Finally, the political nature of education should be recognised by introducing the subject of political education into the curriculum which would involve the teaching of controversial issues.

Uniquely among the writers reviewed here, Nyerere was in a position to attempt to actually implement the changes he set out in *Education for Self-Reliance,* though with varying degrees of success (Harber,1989:Ch.4). However, his criticisms of the nature and purpose of schools in a post-colonial, development context remain relevant as do the reasons for the unsuccessful implementation of some of the policies in practice.

Chapter eleven

Teaching as a Subversive Activity
by Neil Postman and Charles Weingartner
(Harmondsworth: Penguin, 1971)

A teacher in a ghetto school asks a poor, black child, 'How many legs does a grasshopper have? 'Oh man', the child replies, 'I sure wish I had your problems' (joke cited in the book).

Postman and Weingartner, two academic educationalists, start their book by noting the widespread belief in the improvability of the human condition through formal education. Yet, in reality,

"...the way schools are currently conducted does very little, and quite probably nothing, to enhance our chances of mutual survival",

that is, to help us solve the many problems thrown up by constant and rapid change. In fact, the ubiquitous and accelerating pace of social, economic, political, scientific and technological change is the backdrop to the main thesis of the book, that current patterns of formal schooling are irrelevant and outdated in such rapidly changing contexts. Before setting out to develop their ideas in some detail, the authors make an interesting point in passing – that they have been most influenced in their thinking about education by people who work outside education itself, as inside schools or university departments *"there are insufficient daring and vigorous ideas on which to build a new approach to education".*

The first chapter in the book is simply called 'Crap detecting'. They borrow the term from Ernest Hemingway to stress the importance of developing in young people the skills of social, political and cultural criticism i.e. not to automatically accept as true beliefs and assumptions just because they are dominant ones:

"We are, after all, talking about achieving a high degree of freedom from the intellectual and social constraints of one's tribe. For example, it is generally assumed that people of other tribes have been victimised by indoctrination from which our tribe has remained free".

The reason that schools need to become 'training centres for subversion' in the sense of critical questioning is that the for the first time in human history we are living in a time when the pace of change is so fast that accepted knowledge becomes obsolete very rapidly and we simply cannot predict what knowledge will be useful in the future i.e. the nature of change has changed and this has major implications for learning:

"If you are over twenty-five years of age, the mathematics you were taught in school is 'old'; the grammar is obsolete and in disrepute; the biology completely out of date and the history open to serious question. The best that can be said of you, assuming you remember most of what you were told and read, is that you are a walking encyclopedia of outdated information".

Yet what children are mostly asked to do in classrooms is still to sit and listen to the teacher, to believe in authorities and tests and, most of all, to remember: "It is practically unheard of for students to play any role in determining what problems are worth studying or what procedures of enquiry ought to be used". Rather teachers ask questions they think are important: What is the principal river of Uruguay? Why did Brutus betray Caesar? What is the real meaning of this poem? So, what students mostly do is guess what the teacher wants them to say – to supply the Right Answer. What do students primarily learn from this?

- Passive acceptance is a more desirable response to ideas that active criticism.
- Discovering knowledge is beyond the power of students and is, in any case, none of their business.
- Recall is the highest form of intellectual achievement, and the collection of unrelated 'facts' is the goal of education.
- The voice of authority is to be trusted and valued more than independent judgement.
- One's own ideas and those of one's classmates are inconsequential.
- Feelings are irrelevant in education.
- There is always a single, unambiguous Right Answer to a question.
- English is not history and history is not science and science is not art and art is not music, and art and music are minor subjects and English history and science major subjects, and a subject is something you 'take' and, when you have taken it, you have 'had' it, and if you have 'had' it, you are immune and need not take it again.

They describe this as the 'Vaccination Theory of Education' but also later refer to the importance of the concept of 'ventriloquising' in schooling i.e. saying back to the teacher what he or she or a text book has already said, so that no real thinking occurs.

Thus schooling resembles a giant quiz show based on certain answers in a very uncertain world:

"No teacher ever said: 'Don't value uncertainty and tentativeness. Don't question questions. Above all, don't think'. The message is communicated quietly, insidiously, relentlessly and effectively through the structure of the classroom; through the role of the teacher, the role of the student, the rules of their verbal game, the rights that are assigned, the arrangements for communication, the 'doings' that

are praised or censured. In other words, the medium is the message".

Schooling therefore bears a striking similarity to industrial mass production - a five day week, seven hour day, one hour for lunch, careful division of labour for both teachers and students, a high premium on conformity and a corresponding suspicion of originality. As they show, the school curriculum was cogently criticised for being irrelevant and stifling in the 1930s, though exactly the same criticism could be made when they were writing at the end of the 1960s. The exception to this, of course, is students from advantaged backgrounds for whom the curriculum and schooling is relevant in the sense that sticking with it brings certain tangible pay offs. However, as they also point out, but do not develop, the curriculum is insensitive to both gender and ethnicity and does not necessarily suit children with learning difficulties. In the latter case, they make the telling point that if such children are not doing well at school, then this is less of a problem with the children themselves than with the ecology of the school environment.

Teacher education is also part of the problem. The problem is that student teachers have themselves in school been victims for 16 years of *"...servitude in a totalitarian environment ostensibly for the purpose of training them to be fully functioning, self-renewing citizens of a democracy".* Indeed, they are among the most successful at this type of schooling:

"That is they are the ones who learned best what they were required to do: to sit quietly, to accept without question whatever nonsense was inflicted on them, to ventriloquize on demand with a high degree of fidelity, to go down only on the down staircase, to speak only at a signal from the teacher and so on. All during these 16 years, they learned not to think, not to ask questions, not to figure things out for themselves".

So what is necessary in teacher education is to help students to unlearn all their assumptions about what schooling should look like and they must do it by experiencing the kind of education required in schools in the future in their own teacher education. It would do this by shifting the prospective teacher into the role of inventor of viable new teaching strategies and by confronting the student teacher with problems and questions on why they are doing teacher education, what it is supposed to be good for and how they can tell. Some honest answers they have received to the question 'Why am I a teacher?' have included,

- I can control people
- I can tyrannise people
- I have captive audiences
- I have my summers off
- I love seventeenth century non-dramatic Elizabethan literature
- The pay is good, considering the amount of work I actually do.

As they comment, *"Obviously, none of these answers is very promising for the future of our children"*. The authors themselves used ideas from Carl Rogers (discussed later in this book) to confront the students with ideas and beliefs in direct contradiction to the ones they held, and then explaining that they had no planned curriculum for them other than an inquiry into their own largely unexamined beliefs and assumptions.

Instead of a fundamentally authoritarian system of schooling, Postman and Weingartner put forward in some detail an alternative inquiry-method based on the developed skill of asking open–ended questions among learners, exploring a range of possible answers, going wherever the question leads and encouraging student-student interaction. They happily acknowledge that this would be the end of the formal curriculum planned by governments and teachers, but argue that most significant learning processes do not occur in linear, compartmentalised sequences. Indeed, even with a standardised, centralised curriculum, the way each learner receives and tries to make sense of it is highly individualised and messy anyway, even if it looks neat, tidy and coherent to the teacher. Learners are 'meaning makers' whether schools like it or not and it would be better to recognise and facilitate this rather than treat learners as empty buckets to be filled. They also happily recognise the dangers in this from the position of those in authority because once you start people thinking, there is no telling where it will go. Indeed, they contrast the enthusiasm of those in authority for technical educational innovation in the form of, for example, use of TV in the classroom and overhead projectors, and propose a Parkinson's Law of Triviality; the enthusiasm of community leaders for an educational innovation is in inverse proportion to its significance to the learning process.

Their approach would require a new definition of a 'good learner' as a person who:

- Has confidence in their ability to learn
- Enjoys solving problems
- Seems to know what is relevant to their survival and what is not
- Prefers to rely on their own judgement
- Is not fearful of being wrong
- Is not a fast answerer
- Is flexible
- Has a high degree of respect for facts (which they understand are tentative) and can distinguish between these and other kinds of statement
- Is not depressed by the phrase 'I don't know'.

Successful outcomes in this type of education would be in terms of the frequency of questions asked; the increase in relevance and cogency of questions; the frequency and conviction of challenges made to the assertions of other students, teachers and textbooks;

the relevance and clarity of the standards on which they base their challenges; their willingness to suspend judgements when they have insufficient data; their willingness to modify or otherwise change their position when data warrant such a change; the increase in their skill in observing, classifying, generalising etc; the increase in their tolerance to diverse answers and their ability to apply generalisations, attitudes and information to novel situations. Interestingly, in the light of the section on Julius Nyerere above, in order to combat the problems of alienation in city schools, they also propose education with production – that learners should get involved in the production, selling and distribution of goods (clothing, food, household goods) and be evaluated on the basis of these activities rather than on the basis of grades in conventional subjects.

As they summarise at the end of the book, the students who currently endure formal education come out as 'passive acquiescent, dogmatic, intolerant, authoritarian, inflexible, conservative personalities, who desperately need to resist change in an effort to keep their illusion of certainty intact. It would be difficult to imagine any kind of education less liable to help students to meet a drastically changing future'. What is required instead is an education that helps to produce people who are actively enquiring, flexible, creative, innovative, tolerant, liberal and who can face uncertainty and ambiguity without disorientation...'

Chapter twelve

School is Dead
by Everett Reimer
(Harmondsworth:Penguin, 1971)

Reimer begins with the proposition that providing schooling for all globally is expensive and he questions whether the type of school on offer is worth the global effort. Indeed, it may do more harm than good, given that school requires conformity for survival and, for success, the ability to understand the rules and play and win the game on somebody else's terms so that *"the main thing children learn in school is how to lie"*.

For Reimer schools have four distinct social functions. The first is custodial or childcare. He notes that it has been argued that everything a high-school graduate is taught in twelve years in schooling could easily be taught in two years and, with a little effort, in one. But this would be to miss one of the key functions of schooling, that of providing an alternative means of childcare to the family. This childcare function is reflected in the amount of time that schools spend on non-teaching and learning tasks, such as behaviour control, extra-curricular activities and administrative routine, and results from the economic and social function that schools serve as a massive daycare centre for parents who need to go out to work or who are reluctant to spend all day with their offspring. Not only is this a costly form of state-provided childcare but the result is that young people as full-time students remain children economically, politically and legally dependent for longer and longer periods. Thus schooling has become, like armies, prisons and insane asylums, one of society's 'total institutions', though *"strictly speaking, total institutions are those which totally control the lives of their inmates, and even armies, prisons and asylums do this completely only for certain inmates. Only vacation-less boarding schools could strictly be called total institutions, but perhaps the strict definition gives too much attention to the body and too little to the mind and spirit. Schools pervade the lives and personalities of their students in powerful and insidious ways and have become the dominant institution in the lives of modern people during their most formative years".*

The second function is the sorting of the young into slots they will occupy in adult life – allocation to a differential labour market. Different schools and universities provide different occupational life chances to individuals and the education system is therefore one of losers as well as winners. While this may have the outward appearance of being based on merit and equal opportunity, it is in reality largely reproductive of existing social and economic inequalities:

"What schools define as merit is principally the advantage of having literate parents, books in the home, the opportunity to travel etc. Merit is a smoke screen for the perpetuation of privilege".

The third function of schools is indoctrination:

"Indoctrination is a bad word. Bad schools, we say, indoctrinate. Good ones teach basic values. All schools, however, teach the value of childhood, the value of competing for the life prizes offered in school and the value of being taught – not learning for one's self – what is good and what is true. In fact, all schools indoctrinate in ways more effective than those which have generally be recognised. By the time they go to school, children have learned how to use their bodies, how to use language and how to control their emotions. They have learned to depend on themselves and have been rewarded for initiative in learning. In schools these values are reversed. The

what, when, where and how of learning are decided by others, and children learn that it is good to depend on others for their learning. They learn that what is worthwhile is taught and, conversely, that if something is important someone must teach it to them".

The fourth function is to teach cognitive skills. However,

"cognitive learning, although it is declared the principal purpose of schools, occurs only in so far as resources remain after the (other three) in-built functions are performed...some true educational experiences are bound to occur in schools. They occur, however, despite and not because of school".

Reimer points out that one of the defences of schools is: 'Where else would children learn to read?' but according to census data, there are always more literate people than persons who have gone to school, and there are always people who have gone to school and cannot read (or do maths) – and many that can read well and count by the time they get to school. He quotes Einstein commenting on a short period he had to spend in school preparing for a degree examination to the effect that, as a consequence, he was, for several years afterwards, unable to do any creative work.

According to Reimer, schools treat people and knowledge the way a technological world treats everything – as if they could be processed as things. But the price of processing people is high. Many will resist but

"the greatest danger, however, lies in the prospect of success. A successfully processed humanity would lose the little control of its destiny which has always distinguished people from the rest of the world".

So, the whole theory of schooling is based on the assumption that production methods applied to learning will result in learning – they do result in learning how to produce and consume – so long as nothing fundamental changes. Indeed,

"schools learned long ago that the way to keep children from thinking is to keep them busy".

Part of this stopping children from thinking comes from a reluctance to deal with current controversial issues in the classroom, however much children are interested in the topics:

"Schools are obviously as much designed to keep children from learning what really intrigues them as to teach them what they ought to know. As a result children learn to read and do not read, learn their numbers but hate mathematics, shut themselves off in classrooms and do their learning in cloakrooms, hangouts and on the road".

The problem for Reimer is not one of motivating people to learn what others want them to learn. It is rather to provide the resources which enable them to learn what they want and need to know.

Instead of the current system Reimer suggests the following:

- Monopolies in education should be avoided – the school system must not be replaced by another dominant system and alternatives must be plural.
- There should be competition between alternatives but some of them, at least, should not involve competition between students, especially for lifetime prizes.
- One student should not learn at the expense of another, nor should success for one student imply failure for another.
- Alternatives to schools should not manipulate individuals but, on the contrary, should

prepare individuals to direct and re-create institutions.

- Education should not be separated from work and the rest of life but should be integrated with them.

Above all, alternatives to school must allow everyone the opportunity to learn what they need to know in order to act intelligently in their own interests:

"One of the major complications arises from the almost universal predilection to feel that we know better than others what is in their interests. Schools, for example, are almost wholly concerned with trying to teach some people what other people want them to know".

However, in the light of Reimer's point about the increasing custodial or childcare function of schooling, in the final section on 'What each of us can do' he concludes by arguing that

"perhaps the most important single thing that individuals can do is to take back responsibility for the education of their children. Children learn from very young how power is used by the strong in their relations with the weak and it is at least possible that this early learning shapes the individual's behaviour in all their subsequent relations with those who are stronger in the world than they are".

Chapter thirteen

Freedom to Learn
by Carl Rogers
(Columbus: Charles E.Merrill Publishing
Company,1983)

The original version of this book was published in
1969 but here I am using a revised edition from
1983. Rogers starts his book with a quotation from
Einstein:

*"It is in fact nothing short of a miracle that the
modern methods of instruction have not yet entirely
strangled the holy curiosity of inquiry; for this delicate
little plant, aside from stimulation, stands mainly in
need of freedom; without this it goes to wrack and
ruin without fail".*

He accuses the educational system of failing to meet
the real needs of society and argues that schools

*"...constitute the most traditional, conservative, rigid,
bureaucratic institution of our time and the institution
most resistant to change".*

His aim for education, on the other hand, is to
produce effective and concerned citizens, well
informed, competent in knowledge and skills and
confident in facing the future. In order to do this, he
argues, there is a need to help young people learn
how to learn through a process of facilitation of
learning. This stands in contrast to the current
emphasis on the 'basics' and teaching children to
obey and follow rather than be exposed to, and
discuss, controversial social issues and problems and
make choices for themselves. As he warns, *"People
who can't think are ripe for dictatorships".*

He summarises the general purposes of the book as aiming toward:

- A climate of trust in the classroom in which curiosity and the natural desire to learn can be nourished and enhanced.
- Participatory modes of decision-making in all aspects of learning in which students, teachers and administrators each have a part.
- Helping students to prize themselves, to build confidence and self-esteem.
- Uncovering the excitement in intellectual and emotional discovery, which leads students to become life-long learners.
- Developing in teachers the attitudes that research has shown to be most effective in facilitating learning.
- Helping teachers to grow as persons, finding rich satisfaction in their interaction with learners.
- An awareness that, for all of us, the good life is within, not something which is dependent on outside sources.

Rogers begins by examining some of the discouraging aspects of schooling that are obstacles to someone who wants to promote and facilitate learning. One is the degree to which schools are regulated and controlled by outside government bodies. He quotes one teacher as summing up the situation:

"There are stupid piles of paperwork or administrative duties which interfere with the real job in the classroom…Teaching no longer offers the chance to be creative and stimulating. It's frustrating not to be able to try something different. How can you be a teacher without being creative? I feel angry when I feel stifled, not able to use everything I've learned…The students are not robots nor are the teachers, but with the demands of society for budget cuts and higher test scores, we are failing to recognise that we are dealing with students who are feeling, total, human

beings...People are so afraid of creativity because that might cause change and undermine their sense of security. I really want to help my students find a sense of security within themselves so that the inevitable change will not scare them. One thing we had better learn to cope with is change!"

Rogers identifies a particular threat as coming from right-wing political forces in terms of their believing in a 'right' view which is to be taught and accepted, and where those in authority select school content, and discourage free and open discussion of complex problems and the consideration of a range of alternative ways forward in favour of their stance on morality.

He also argues that there is widespread evidence of dissatisfaction among students in schools (and universities) because of being lectured to boredom, and the stressful pressure of the increasing emphasis on grades and examinations. He adds that in 1981 the President of Yale stated that 'America cannot allow itself to transform the public schools into warehouses for the angry' and comments that this is a good description of many schools – warehouses for the bored, the unhappy and the angry. While he recognises that there are positive and exciting exceptions,

"I think I have said quite enough to indicate that our educational system is suffering from many elements of a crippling sort: the decreased financial resources, the dwindling enrolment, the tangled web of law and bureaucratic regulations that so often dehumanises the classroom, a dangerous right-wing attack that aims to prevent freedom of thought and choice, and boredom, frustration, rage and despair on the part of many students...we are locked into a traditional and conventional approach that makes significant learning improbable if not impossible. When we put together in one scheme such elements as a prescribed curriculum, similar assignments for all students,

lecturing as almost the only mode of instruction, standard tests by which all students are externally evaluated, and instructor-chosen grades as the measure of learning, then we can almost guarantee meaningful learning will be at a minimum".

Commenting of the feelings of some student teachers about their own schooling, he notes that they are almost all negative and even the positive feelings have to do with escaping from school:

"Their experience has been composed of fear, failure, humiliation, resentment, constriction. These are the important learnings – the personal ones. The content of their courses – what they were supposed to have learned – doesn't even come to mind! What an incredible fact! We have paid our taxpayers' money in order to have our children scarred, damaged, hurt, and stultified – changed from eager learners into active rebels against education...Why do we, as a community, continue to insist on a school experience that damages, when a proven alternative exists?"

Moreover, teacher education institutions are part of the problem as

"they tend to be rigid bastions of conventional thinking and practice, and highly resistant to change. On many university campuses, education courses are looked upon as a boring waste of time".

To summarise, Rogers characterises the traditional, 'mug and jug' mode of education as follows:

- The teacher is the possessor of knowledge, the student the expected recipient.
- The lecture, the textbook or some other means of verbal intellectual instruction are the major methods of getting knowledge into the recipient. The examination measures the extent to which the student has received it.

- The teacher is the possessor of power, the student the one who obeys.
- Rule by authority is the accepted policy in the classroom.
- Trust is at a minimum.
- The subjects (students) are best governed by being kept in an intermittent or constant state of fear.
- Democracy and its values are ignored and scorned in practice.
- There is no place for the whole person in the educational system, only for her intellect.

Whereas these characteristics tend to be seen as inevitable, Rogers asks whether alternatives are possible – starting with the question 'Can We Be Human in the Classroom?' – and provides many concrete and detailed examples where teachers and learners collaborate in setting the goals, methods and content of learning with the teacher as facilitator. These, he argues, are not confined to specific subjects or situations but are about a person-centred way of being in any educational situation:

"It is a set of values, not easy to achieve, placing emphasis on the dignity of the individual, the importance of personal choice, the significance of responsibility, the joy of creativity. It is a philosophy built on a foundation of the democratic way of empowering each individual".

This is important because of the ever-changing nature of the world and the changing nature of knowledge and understanding. Hence the importance of learning to learn and the encouragement of self-reliant learners because no knowledge is absolutely secure for all time. The best, therefore, that teachers can and should do is facilitation of this process of developing self-reliant learners, to trust learners and act as a catalyst of learning. Such a facilitator of learning begins by asking questions such as:

- What do you want to learn?
- What things puzzle you?
- What are you curious about?
- What issues concern you?
- What problems do you wish you could solve?

This necessitates facilitators asking themselves how they can create a learning climate in which children will feel free to be curious, will feel free to make mistakes, will feel free to learn from the environment, from fellow students, from themselves and from experience. In answer to the accusation that such individualised or personalised learning is impractical because it would involve an enormous increase in the number teachers, he argues that

"nothing could be further from the truth. For one thing, when children are eager to learn, they follow up their own leads and engage in a great deal of independent study of their own. There is also a great saving of the teacher's time because problems of discipline or control drop tremendously".

And children help each other to learn. One teacher told Rogers that in fact she had more time to spend with each child, not less, when she set each child free to learn. Therefore,

"I deeply believe that traditional teaching is an almost completely futile, wasteful, overrated function in today's changing world. It is successful mostly in giving children who can't grasp the material, a sense of failure".

Rogers summarises the person-centred mode of education as follows:

- The precondition is: a leader or a person who is perceived as an authority figure in the situation is sufficiently secure within herself and in her relationships to others that she experiences an essential trust in the capacity of others to think for themselves.

- The facilitative teacher shares with others – students, and possibly also parents and community members – the responsibility for the learning process.
- The facilitator provides learning resources, from within herself and her own experience, from books or materials or community experiences.
- The student develops her own programme of learning, alone or in cooperation with others.
- A facilitative learning climate is provided.
- The focus is primarily on fostering the continuing process of learning.
- The discipline necessary to reach the student's goals is a self-discipline.
- The evaluation of the extent and significance of the student's learning is made primarily by the learner.
- In this growth-promoting climate, the learning tends to be deeper, proceed at a more rapid rate, and is more pervasive in the life and behaviour of the student than is learning acquired in the traditional classroom.

Rogers reviews evidence from America and Europe which strongly suggests that students learn more, attend school more often and are more creative and capable of problem solving when this kind of education is experienced.

He concludes the book with some final observations about what a small boy pupil learns on his first day at school:

- There is no place for his restless physical energy in the school room.
- One conforms or takes the unpleasant consequences.
- Submission to rules is very important.
- Making a mistake is very bad.

- The punishment for a mistake is humiliation.
- Spontaneous interest does not belong in a school.
- Teacher and disciplinarian are synonymous.
- School is, on the whole, an unpleasant experience.

As time goes on, he learns further things:

- Most textbooks are boring.
- It is not safe to differ with a teacher.
- It is OK to cheat.
- Daydreams and fantasies can make the day pass more quickly.
- To study hard and get good grades is behaviour scorned by his peers.
- Most of the learning relevant to life takes place outside the school.
- Original ideas have no place in school.
- Exams and grades are the most important aspects of education.
- Most teachers are, in class, impersonal and boring.

On the other hand, a small girl goes to a school where they sit in a circle with the teacher and discuss what they are interested in and they would like to do. There are lots of interesting things in the room and the teacher's interest in the pupils is evident. This pupil has begun to learn that:

- Her curiosity is welcomed and prized.
- The teacher is friendly and caring.
- She can learn new things, both on her own and with the teacher's help.
- She can contribute to group learning.
- She is valued as a person.

As she continues at her more humanistically oriented school:

- She will play a part in choosing what she wishes and needs to learn.

- She will learn reading and mathematics more rapidly than her friends in other schools.
- She will find at outlet for her creativity.
- She will become more expressive of both feelings and thoughts.
- She will develop a confidence in, and liking for, herself.
- She will discover that learning is fun.
- She will look forward to going to school.
- She will like and respect her teachers and will be liked and respected in turn.
- She will find a place in school for all her many and expanding interests.
- She will develop a knowledge of resources, ways of finding out what she wants to know.
- She will read, think about and discuss crucial social issues of her time.
- She will find some things very difficult to learn, requiring effort, concentration and self-discipline.
- She finds such learning very rewarding.
- She learns to attack a task cooperatively, working with others to achieve a goal.
- She is on the way to becoming an educated person, one who is learning how to learn.

At present, according to Rogers, formal education systems tend to create conformists and followers because those with power are reluctant to share it with the group for which they are all responsible – the learners. Instead of 'no taxation without representation' he suggests 'no curriculum without student participation' so as to put a democratic philosophy of education into action in the classroom. He ends the book by saying, "It all boils down to the question we must ask, both individually and collectively: Do we dare?"

Chapter fourteen

Key Critiques

As argued in the introduction to this book, in dominant discourses on education globally, schooling is still most often automatically assumed to be good for learners and for society. These writers did not agree. What, then, are the key criticisms of schooling emerging from these books?

- Schools are authoritarian institutions with little serious participation by pupils in decision-making and particularly in curriculum, teaching and learning.
- Schooling is increasingly controlled from above and therefore rigid, bureaucratic and based on the principle of one-size-fits-all rather than flexible and able to meet the needs of individuals.
- A fixed, subject-based, official curriculum does not, and cannot, educate for the rapidly changing present, let alone the future.
- Much of what is taught in school is not perceived as relevant, interesting or useful by learners.
- Schooling is often based on compulsion to attend which, given the nature of schooling, both creates problems of resistance and ignores valid alternatives.
- Many, though not all, children are unhappy and bored at school.
- Schooling is driven by tests, examinations and 'right answers' which dictate the nature of classroom activity and cause stress and harm to pupils.
- Teacher education is part of the problem as, rather than challenging what happens in

schools, it tends to socialise for it and reproduce it.

- Schooling is more about the reproduction of social inequalities than the provision of equality of opportunity – and this is so both within nations and between nations.
- Corporal punishment is harmful to learning and must go.
- Schooling tends to avoid critical and creative discussion of controversial issues.
- It is often forgotten that schooling is, historically, a relatively recent form of education and that there are other forms. However, the essentials of schooling have not altered significantly since its origins.
- Schooling serves important functions other than genuine education such as socialisation and indoctrination, freeing adults to contribute to, and earn from, the labour market and creating a source of employment of educational professionals.
- A great deal of time in schools is wasted.
- There is a great deal of 'do as I say' from adults in schools rather than 'do as I do'.

Chapter fifteen

Schooling Today: Much the Same?

"Schools are havens of peace in a troubled world", David Wylde, President of the International Confederation of School Principals (O'Malley 2005).

"We have to note that, unfortunately, education has not always and in all circumstances served to liberate people from the barriers of ignorance. It hasn't always helped them to affirm their dignity nor to map their own destiny freely. It has also served, and continues to do so, to bolster ruling elites, to exclude and even, it has to be said, to ferment conflicts. And this is precisely because education is not just a means of acquiring knowledge but also a vehicle for moral and ideological training available to any social organization", Koichiro Matsuura, Director General of the United Nations (cited in Osler and Starkey 2005:34).

As the above quotations suggest, opinions differ on the contemporary role of schooling. The rest of this book examines, first in this section, whether the critiques of schooling made in the texts reviewed above still hold true and then, second in the following section, whether the situation is actually worse than the negative picture of schooling that they painted thirty or forty years ago.

Authoritarianism, Control and Curriculum

I begin this section with a case study of one former pupil. In *Stupid White Men* former pupil Michael Moore is less than complementary about his schooling in America. His description of his primary schooling contains phrases like *"My dislike of schooling started somewhere around the second month of first grade"* and "*I was bored beyond belief*" but it got even worse at junior secondary school: "*High school, as we know, is some sort of sick, sadistic punishment of kids by adults seeking vengeance because they can no longer lead the responsibility-free, screwing around lives young people enjoy. What other explanation could there be for those four brutal years of degrading comments, physical abuse...those running the public high school system had one simple mission: 'Hunt the little pricks down like dogs, then cage them until we can break their will or ship them off to the glue factory'. Do this, don't do that, tuck your shirt in, wipe that smile off you face, where's your hall pass, THAT'S THE WRONG PASS! YOU – DETENTION!!*" (Moore,2001:95-97)

One of the accusations made by the books summarised here is that schooling is an authoritarian institution, largely unsuitable for providing young people with the experience of democracy they require to help them to become more democratic citizens. The conclusion is either they need reforming in a more democratic direction or to be replaced by other forms of learning that are more democratic. However, despite much discussion of the possibilities of democratic education, including those by the writer himself, the dominant form of schooling worldwide remains authoritarian. While the degree of harshness and despotism within schools varies from context to context and from institution to institution, in the majority of schools power over what is taught and learned, how it is taught and learned, where it is taught and learned, when it is taught and learned and what the general learning environment is like is not in the hands of pupils. It is predominantly government officials, headteachers and teachers who decide, not learners. Most schools are essentially authoritarian institutions, however benevolent or benign that authoritarianism is and whatever beneficial aspects of learning are imparted.

In *Schooling As Violence* (2004), and despite acknowledging exceptions, I reviewed evidence from six major geographical regions (Africa, Asia, Europe, the Middle East, North America and South and Central America) that confirmed authoritarianism as the hegemonic international model of schooling which was deeply rooted in the original, historical purposes of schooling and thus impervious to substantial change. However, in their global report on 'Education for All by 2015' UNESCO note that

"...national policies indicate a trend to revise curricula to make classroom interactions more responsive and centred on the child. There is a move away from traditional 'chalk and talk' teaching to more discovery-based learning and a greater emphasis on outcomes that are broader than basic recall of facts and information" (UNESCO,2008:131).

They note that such policies are 'encouraging', a sign that any real change on a broader and lower level is yet to happen to any significant degree. Internationally, I have been reading about such encouraging intentions at the educational policy level for most of my professional life but the dominant reality on the ground never seems to change in any significant or meaningful way. Even societies seemingly committed at the policy level to democratic change in schooling, such as South Africa, find that it is much harder to change authoritarian realities on the ground in a sustainable manner (see, for example, Nelson Mandela Foundation 2005; Karlsson 2002; Fiske and Ladd 2004; Fataar 2007; Hunt 2007).

In England, despite a growth in school councils dealing with other matters, pupils still have very little say over the core purpose of schooling - curriculum and teaching and learning methods. Indeed, in many ways the introduction of a subject aimed at education for democratic citizenship has merely highlighted gaps between the stated aims and practices of this area and the rest of what happens in schooling in terms of a centrally prescribed curriculum, testing and competitive league tables (Harber 2009 a and b). The effects of twenty years of the national curriculum have also begun to be openly noticed and discussed. A report by academics at Cambridge University argued that the centralised and prescriptive culture of curriculum control, targets and initiatives had stifled creativity and spontaneity among teachers (Marley 2008a). At the same time a lengthy article in the *Times Higher Education Supplement* (10/1/2008) argued that in the exam-driven, pass at all costs context of school league tables, pupils are spoon-fed information. The result is a lack of experience of the independent and critical thinking required when they get to university. This debate re-surfaced in the columns of the twin publication the *Times Educational Supplement* where a Professor of Behavioural Ecology at Sheffield University complained that:

"The most striking thing about undergraduates is their dependence, their lack of initiative and their reluctance to think for themselves...New undergraduates expect to be told what to do at every stage. It is almost as though the spoon-feeding-and-teaching-to-the-test culture has drained them of independence of thought" (Birkhead 2009).

Subsequent correspondents (13/2) agreed and argued that also responsible was the dominance of screen-based Information Communications Technology (ICT), a concomitant decline in reading, the tick-box commodification of children's learning experience and cramming information into children in as short a time as possible in order to pass 'fact'-based exams. One ended his letter, which drew parallels with a previous article about entire GCSE courses being taught in 60 minutes, by commenting,

"I doubt that many teachers would have been moved to join the profession if they had been shown banks of

children hooked up to computers, reciting the elements of the periodic table like drones from George Orwell's 1984".

In very recent years there have been two major reports in England (by Robin Alexander in 2009 and Sir Jim Rose in 2008) which have begun to talk more openly about 're-designing' the education system to be less driven by a rigid, subject-based national curriculum and more based on personalised learning, thematic areas of understanding, pupil participation, cooperation, and flexibility (as though these are sensational news items and radically new ideas). However, the reality is that so far there has been relatively little dismantling of the centralised educational apparatus set up by the Conservative government in the Reform Act of 1988. Moreover, it appears quite possible that a Conservative government overtly opposed to 'progressive teaching' will be returned to power by 2010 (Curtis 2008a).

In some countries this authoritarianism is reflected in a growing compulsion to attend, which exceeds the situation in the 1960s and 1970s. In England parents are sent to prison if a child plays truant, police patrols search for school refusers and head teachers propose to fine parents up to £100 for taking their children away on holiday in term time without permission. There are serious discussions about, and even trial runs of, the use of electronic tagging devices to cut down truancy in America, Japan and Britain (Lee 2005). A letter from a parent in Birmingham that appeared in *The Guardian* newspaper (2/3/2009) said:

"It is reassuring to know that an informed Whitehall security adviser believes gathering confidential data should depend on 'the seriousness of the business in hand'. Could Sir David possibly have a word with the people running my 11-year-old daughter's school?

Because they've asked to scan her fingerprints before serving her food at lunchtime".

In America there is a growing trend of criminalization of student misbehaviour. School discipline cases concerning matters such as violations of the school dress codes and being loud and disruptive in school are increasingly being sent to the courts and the juvenile justice system rather than being handled by the principal's office. One girl who refused to abide by the dress code was handcuffed by a city police officer and taken in a police car to a detention centre. In Ohio, Virginia, Kentucky and Florida juvenile court judges are complaining that their courtrooms are at risk of being overwhelmed by student misconduct cases that should be handled in schools. One juvenile court judge talked of the 'demonising of children' (Rimer 2004). A head teacher in South Carolina resigned amid public pressure after agreeing to a commando-style police raid in which officers stormed classes, guns drawn, handcuffing and pinning students to the floor in a futile drugs search (Phillips 2006). Moreover, although schooling is perceived as 'compulsory' in many countries (it isn't necessarily, though education usually is), it is also far from free. Many schools globally, including those in relatively poor countries, charge fees (UNESCO,2008:112) and in all countries there are many hidden costs to schooling such as travel, uniform, books and extracurricular activities.

This authoritarianism is also a reflection of the degree of control exercised in educational systems. In reflecting on his detailed empirical five nation study of culture and pedagogy Alexander (2000) was struck by the pervasive sense of control in all five schooling systems – America, England, France, India and Russia. The controlling function is exercised at different levels:

"At national level (or state level in the United States) governments devise policies and structures, allocate

budgets, determine goals, define curricula and institute mechanisms for assessing and policing what goes on at the system's lower levels. At regional and local levels such systems may be replicated or, depending on the balance of control over what goes on in the classrooms, they may simply be implemented. At school level, heads exercise varying degrees of influence or direct control over what goes on in classrooms; and at the end of the line, in classrooms, children are every day subjected to the pedagogic controls of teaching and curriculum. These controls extend into the furthest recesses of task, activity and interaction, and are mediated through routine, rule and ritual. Comparative macro-micro analysis illuminates the way these stack up and cumulatively impact on the child...The mechanisms are universal: structure, curriculum, assessment, inspection, qualifications, school organisation and teaching" (Alexander 2000:562).

On the other hand, as noted above, those who do truant are being tracked in ever more sophisticated ways. In Singapore and the UK mobile phones and text messages are being used to contact parents when a child is absent without notification (*Times Educational Supplement* 13/4/2001; *The Guardian* 1/6/2001). In Germany an electronics company has developed a tracker which can be sown into a school uniform or school bag which will use global positioning satellite technology and be able to pinpoint a truanting child to within five metres and alert teachers and parents (Leidig 2000). Recently in England it was announced that children are to be tracked around schools and other sites they visit for lessons via microchips embedded in their uniforms which, not surprisingly, did not go down well with civil liberties groups (Milne 2007).

This degree of authoritarianism and control is no accident. Green (1990) has argued convincingly that a major purpose of the introduction of mass formal schooling systems at the end of the nineteenth century was social and political control, in particular to counter the threat to the state of increasingly industrialised, urbanised and potentially organised working populations. Schooling would be organised to prepare future workers with the subordinate values and behaviours necessary for the modern bureaucratic, mass production workplace and the existing social order – regularity, routine, monotonous work and strict discipline. Its organisational form would therefore need to be authoritarian in order to inculcate habits of obedience and conformity. This authoritarian model of schooling with its origins in state formation, modernisation and social and political control gradually extended globally from European societies and Japan through colonisation where the key purpose of schooling was to help to control indigenous populations for the benefit of the colonial power. By the 1930s colonialism had exercised its sway over 84.6 per cent of the land surface of the globe (Loomba 1998:15). Subsequently, many post-colonial governments did not hesitate to use schooling for purposes of political control (e.g. Harber 1989; Watkins 1999; Brown 2005).

Moreover, historically, authoritarianism was also reflected in the curriculum. Kelly (1986) argues that historically the dominant epistemology or view of knowledge that has influenced curriculum planning is that knowledge is certain, factual and objective rather than contentious and subject to change and interpretation. This view of knowledge stems from European culture at the end of the eighteenth century, the period of the 'Enlightenment', when the aim was to formulate general laws based on observation and experiment. He argues that this stress on certainty and the one 'right' answer leads to authoritarianism. This is because if knowledge is absolute and unchanging then there cannot be legitimate alternatives to it. There is little point in discussion and dialogue as the role of the teacher is to impart a factual body of knowledge to immature recipients. This means a stress on the transmission of cognitive knowledge, subject content and values as though they were facts, rather than education about values, skills, feelings and relationships. It also means an emphasis on teacher-centred learning over enquiry, discussion and critical analysis.

One contemporary legacy of this history, and one obstacle to greater pupil voice in decision making, is the discomfort that many teachers globally feel about discussing controversial issues and values in the classroom and the wider school. As a result, teachers today (and in the 1960s and 1970s according to the criticisms of schooling made by the books reviewed above), are more comfortable with teaching 'facts', information and concepts than encouraging discussion of controversial issues where there are no clear cut 'right answers' and where the purpose of learning is exploration, clarification and enhanced understanding, sometimes of mutually contradictory ideas. There is considerable evidence of this reluctance, for example, in the UK (Davies, Gregory and Riley 1999; Oulton et al 2004; Davies, Yamashita and Harber 2005) and South Africa (Harber 2001:82; Harber and Serf 2006) and one important thread of these findings is that teachers say that they have not been trained to teach controversial issues.

Resistance to Schooling

Pupils have been involved in organised protests against schooling since medieval times. In 1911 up to a million school pupils in Britain went on strike. In other countries too – America, China and South Africa – there have been organised forms of resistance to schooling (Adams 1991). Some pupils react by absenting themselves – in Britain, despite fines and truancy sweeps, truancy rates rose in 2007 so that 60,000 pupils were absent from school without permission every day (TES 9/5/2008). Interestingly, even OFSTED have now said that poor teaching, boring lessons and a rigid curriculum are to blame for rising levels of secondary school truancy (Marley and Hilborne 2007).

In other countries where schooling is not provided for all, there is the problem of drop-out and non-attendance. This may be as much a case of 'push-out' because of the nature of schooling on offer as much as 'drop out' for financial reasons (Harber 2004:Ch.1). For example, a DfID/Save the Children study of schooling in India, Mali, Palestinian camps in Lebanon, Liberia, Mozambique, Pakistan, Mongolia, Ethiopia and Peru stated that, while many people put their faith in schools to offer children a better chance in life, for some,

'the local schools are of such poor quality that it is developmentally healthier for children not to be in them. The school systems are run by inflexible bureaucracies – if children face difficulties in attending because of the constraints of their lives, that is their problem, not one for the school system to sort out. What is taught in school is often incomprehensible (in a language children have never heard) and unrelated to their lives. Teachers are harsh, unmotivated and unmotivating. Children drop out, having learnt little' (Molteno et al 2000:2).

Even those pushing for greater school attendance on a global scale admit that the problem can be with the schools:

"unsafe, overcrowded and poorly equipped schools with inadequately trained teachers contribute to student dropout" (UNESCO 2008).

So, it is perhaps not surprising that, when asked, pupils have some significant criticisms to make of schooling. In 2003 the results of a survey based on Edward Blishen's original *The School That I'd Like* (summarised above) were published, some thirty-six years later. Nothing had fundamentally changed. The foreword to a study of the views of 15,000 pupils on schooling in Britain made some very pertinent points in the light of the findings that followed:

"*How can we turn schools into places where children happily go and are able to learn? And what is education for anyway?...'Respect' was the single word that occurred most; it was what the children wanted but felt they didn't get. They were forced to do work they weren't interested in, in buildings that were falling down around their ears. They were expected to fit into a structure and a curriculum that seemed to have been created without the first reference to what they might enjoy, or respond to. Most of all, they were sick of not being listened to*" (Gardiner 2003:ix-x).

There have been similar findings from studies of pupil views on schooling from America (Cushman 2003), Greece and Spain (UNESCO 2003:5). A study of primary school children in Ireland found that,

"*in general children defined their relationships with their teachers in terms of control and regulation...school was experienced as something that was done to them and over which they exercised little control...The children's talk was replete with examples of adult power. They remarked on the absence of consultation with them over curricular, pedagogical and evaluative practices in schools...adults decided what and how children would learn*" (Devine 2003:138-40).

Fewer studies have been done on pupils' views in developing countries but some academic studies have noted the often rigid, boring, irrelevant and poor quality of the schooling on offer (Molteno et al 2000:2,71; Alexander 2000:9). A study in Indonesia (Wibowo 2005) found that children's views on education are not usually taken into account by researchers or, as the study established, by teachers and educational policy makers:

"...parents and policy makers at all levels make decisions and formulate policies generally on the basis of adult perspectives. Their policies related to children's necessities are mostly focused on the provision and the protection of the children based on adult views, whereas children's right to participation is neglected and remains a formality" (p.190).

One study of rural schools in South Africa did ask pupils about their schooling. It found that there were worse problems than boredom or irrelevance – not only was the teacher-centred classroom still the norm but pupils registered their dislike of the continuing use of corporal punishment and the sexual harassment and abuse of female students (Nelson Mandela Foundation 2005).

Social Reproduction and the Maintenance of Inequalities

The same study noted that,

"For many, education cannot compensate for much deeper economic and social inequalities – it is not a ladder out of poverty, it simply confirms one's status in life" (Nelson Mandela Foundation, 2005:142).

The books reviewed above were strongly critical of the schooling system thirty or forty years ago for masking their role in the reproduction of social inequality by a façade of equality of opportunity and meritocracy. Their case was strengthened by the historical work carried out by Bowles and Gintis (1976) in America. Have matters improved?

If Britain is anything to go by, it would seem not. Two recent large scale studies carried out by Bristol University and Kings College London produced very strong evidence of the continuing significance of social class background in influencing the educational chances of success of pupils in Britain. Children from middle class backgrounds have access to higher quality educational resources and have better prospects of academic achievement than children from poorer backgrounds (Asthana and Hinscliff 2006; Taylor 2006). Research carried out by the Sutton Trust concluded that social mobility in Britain was at a standstill and that social class was still the biggest predictor of school achievement or getting a degree – *"the advantages of being born into a privileged home have not changed in 30 years"* (Curtis 2007a). A study commissioned by the National College of School Leadership and the National Union of Teachers (Mongon and Chapman 2008) suggested that the cycle of white working class underachievement has been endemic since mass education was introduced at the end of the nineteenth century. Family income and status are still by far the most significant correlates of success in the school system. A study by academics at Birmingham University of 12,575 15-year-olds in five European countries, including England, concluded that the secondary school that pupils attended made very little difference to their academic achievement as attainment is largely determined by family background (Bloom 2008).

The British political elite also continues to be dominated by the products of expensive private schools. Whereas 7% of the general population goes to private school, 76% of judges comes from private schools, 68% of barristers, 55% of solicitors, 32% of members of parliament, 42% of party leaders, 56% of life peers in the House of Lords, 56% of top newspaper journalists and 56% of top TV journalists (Garner and Russell 2006). 90% of the most senior army officers were privately educated as were six out of ten in the navy (Oliver and Grimston 2009).

In Africa political elites also utilise expensive private schools to help retain the privileged positions of their families (Boyle 1999). South Africa, in particular, has made an effort to use education to create greater opportunity and equity. Yet the ability of individual schools to set fees has meant that this policy ambition has not been achieved. Schools serving well off communities can charge high fees to maintain excellent facilities and employ more teachers while schools in poorer communities will not be able to do so. Admission on the grounds of race may now be illegal but high fees may well have the same net effect. It seems very likely that public schools will be increasingly divided between a minority of relatively affluent and well resourced schools and a majority of poorer schools much more dependent on state funding. In their detailed study of two provinces tellingly entitled *Elusive Equity*, Fiske and Ladd (2004:233/4) conclude that South Africa has made progress on equal *treatment* in terms of allocation of state resources but the country has been less successful in terms of equal *educational opportunity* because of the very unequal access to good quality schooling, and not successful at all in terms of educational *adequacy* in that repetition and dropout rates among black students remain high and matriculation pass rates low with little evidence of improvement. This is a similar conclusion to that reached by Spreen and Vally (2006:354-7) who also point out that many children go to school hungry and that 27% of schools have no running water, 43% have no electricity, 80% have no library and 78% have no computers. A study of rural schools in South Africa graphically brings home the way poverty both prevents access to education and success within it (Nelson Mandela Foundation 2005).

A study in India also challenged the view that formal education will inevitably undermine established processes of caste and class, concluding that, unless wealth and land is redistributed, formal education can only be partially successful in raising the social standing and economic position of disadvantaged groups. Moreover, throughout the developing world there is evidence that rural people may rapidly withdraw from investing in formal schooling when educated young people fail to find employment. The authors suggest the need to be wary of the assumption – most associated with the work of Amartya Sen – of the potential of formal education to transform lives because the school plays a significant role in reproducing inequality (Jeffrey, Jeffery and Jeffery 2008).

Globally, enormous inequalities in wealth between countries also mean that there is a 'vast gulf' in educational opportunities between young people in richer and poorer countries. The significantly different levels of access and quality mean that, internationally, schooling also helps to reproduce inequality between nations which is why the 2009 global monitoring report on education for all is subtitled 'Overcoming inequality' (UNESCO 2009). Also, *within* developing countries unequal access to education and qualifications helps to reproduce inequality as the following table suggests:

Average Years of Education for Richest and Poorest 20% of 17-22 Year Olds

Richest 20%		Poorest 20%
8.1	Bangladesh	3.7
5.6	Burkino Faso	0.8
7.4	Ethiopia	1.6
9.2	Ghana	3.2
8.3	Guatemala	1.9
11.	India	4.4
4.8	Mali	0.4
5.0	Mozambique	1.9
9.2	Nicaragua	2.5
9.9	Nigeria	3.9
11.1	Peru	6.5
11.0	Philippines	6.3
8.1	Tanzania	3.9
9.0	Zambia	4.0

(Elliott 2008).

As the writer of the article from which these figures are taken acknowledges, the schooling actually provided to the poor is also likely to be of lower quality.

The writers of the books in the 1960s and 1970s summarised above were very aware of the role of schooling in the reproduction of socio-economic status, though less so in terms of ethnicity and gender, fields of sociological study which began to burgeon towards the end of this period. However, these are now also perceived as additional and significant aspects of inequality, though they intersect with economic inequality. In Britain, for example, there has been much research on, and public debate about, the under-achievement of black Caribbean pupils (e.g.DfES 2006; Archer and Francis 2007 Ch.1). Some researchers have even accused English schools of being institutionally racist because teachers routinely underestimate the abilities of some black pupils, though others disagree (Curtis 2008b). Although many possible reasons are put forward for the underachievement of this group of pupils, the fact remains that there is little disagreement on the evidence itself and schooling appears to be doing little to provide greater equality of opportunity in this respect.

In terms of ethnicity, UNESCO recognises that this can be a barrier to access to schooling, and that schooling in many countries can fail to meet the needs of indigenous populations, communicating outside the main imported colonial language and also to children belonging to nomadic or pastoralist communities. It has focused on particular Roma children who face segregation and discrimination in schools in parts of Europe (UNESCO 2008:48,120).

In November 2007 the European Court of Human Rights in Strasbourg found the Czech Republic guilty of racism and discrimination against the Roma or gypsy minority for dumping their children in 'special schools' for those with learning difficulties and segregating schools and classes between Roma and Czechs. Findings from Amnesty International and the Open Society Institute confirm similar discrimination in Slovakia. The OSI study found that Roma children in Slovakia are 28 times more likely to be put in special schools than non-Roma children and in the Czech Republic, 27 times more likely (Traynor 2007).

The South African Human Rights Commission Report was an audit of 90 desegregated schools across all nine provinces (Vally and Dalamba 1999) showed that racism in schools was pervasive. They summarised the situation as follows:

"In fact little progress has been made to ensure an end to racial discrimination and prejudice in schools. Our Commission has had to deal with a large number of complaints: discrimination in disciplinary measures, racial violence and cultural prejudice. Schools continue to be characterised by racial separation and discrimination. Efforts at racial integration have not achieved the desired results because learners approach school with the prejudices imbued in their home environments and the schools have no mechanisms to challenge and stimulate the unlearning of ingrained prejudices, as well as transform the minds of learners. Educators exhibit little or no commitment to constructing a learning environment free from discrimination and prejudice. Too many prefer to deny the existence of racism or presume a superficial tolerance. Some prefer to have their schools as laboratories for cultural assimilation where black learners are by and large tolerated rather than affirmed as of right. Four years after the miracle of 1994, school playgrounds are battlegrounds between black and white school goers" (1999:Preface).

A recent study of a community near Cape Town sheds

some interesting light on how education continues to reproduce racial separation and antagonism in South Africa. The researcher found that both 'coloured' and 'black' parents and children had negative stereotypes of each other but that school did little to combat this situation. The national language policy prescribing that children be taught in their mother tongue in the first three grades meant that almost no racial integration took place in those grades. This also affected mixing among teachers with at least one school having a separate common room for each ethnic/linguistic group. Most teachers expressed exasperation at having to commit to adopting an anti-racist pedagogy and effectively turned a blind eye to the racial antagonisms displayed by parents in and out of school. Indeed, most of the churches and cultural and sports groupings that used the schools' facilities also did so on the basis of race (Fataar 2007). In her study of four schools that had been differently racially categorised under apartheid Hunt (2007 Ch.7) found that the schools had done little to embrace a new culture actively based on non-discrimination and equality but that students not from the dominant group had been expected to assimilate into existing practices and discourses.

As regards gender inequality, in Britain females have caught up and overtaken males in terms of achievement in examinations in some areas since the era that the reviewed books were published, though there are still significant differences according to subjects, universities attended and entrance to teacher education, and men also still tend to predominate in the professions and in senior employment positions (Meighan and Harber, 2007:Ch.26). So, while there is now greater gender equality within schooling than there was, there are still some important gender differences in the educational experience, and traditional links to patterns of employment in terms of type of job and level of job seem to have been less affected.

While gender remains an issue in British schools (e.g. Francis and Skelton 2005; Jackson 2006; Pinker 2008), elsewhere in the world the problems remains more stark. In 2005 only about one-third of 181 countries had achieved gender parity in terms of access to school. Textbooks in many countries remain gender biased and, while the academic performance of girls and boys is converging, as in the UK, fields of study and occupational choices remain clustered by gender. As also in the UK, there are starting to be worries about boys performance in schools. However, within the school boys' generally enjoy more challenging interactions with teachers, dominate classroom activities and receive more attention than girls. Teachers also often have different expectations of boys and girls, with teachers seeing girls as succeeding through quiet diligence and hard work and boys as more 'naturally clever' (UNESCO 2008:79-89).

Finally, corruption in education is an issue confronting social equality in many countries. As a recent book on corruption in schools and universities in a range of countries puts it, there is no lack of data illustrating the diverse forms that corruption can take in the education sector (Hallak and Poisson 2006). As the authors of this book also point out, educational corruption and malpractice undermine one of the main potentially positive purposes of education, the promotion of universal values including integrity, citizenship and ethics. A report by Save the Children in Mongolia, for example, noted that teachers had started hidden businesses forcing pupils to buy textbooks, handouts and charging illegal fees thus pricing out many from attending school. This, incidentally, is also coupled with widespread physical and emotional violence against children by teachers in school, and is also a major disincentive to attend (Save the Children 2006).

So, at the very least, the criticism that schooling

reproduces social inequality rather than helping to reduce it continues to have very many grains of truth in it.

Exams and Testing

One significant factor in the authoritarian, teacher-led nature of schooling, pupils' resistance to schooling and social and economic reproduction that was noted in many of the texts reviewed above, was the dominating and domineering role of tests and examinations. I have discussed in some detail both British and international evidence of the educational, physical and mental harm (including suicide) done to pupils by over-testing and examinations, often primarily for the benefit of the state rather than the learner (Harber 2004:Ch.8). In most countries the situation does not seem to have improved much in the thirty or forty years since these books were written, and in England at least the situation has become worse. In England, while the prominence of the testing regime certainly does not seem to have changed since 2004, more and more people, some in positions of authority, are noticing its detrimental effects. The primary review based at the University of Cambridge made the comparative point that 'What distinguishes assessment policy in England is the degree to which it is used as a tool to control what is taught and police how well it is taught' (www.primaryreview.ork.uk; Bloom and Ward 2008). Even members of the House of Commons seem to have noticed. The Commons Committee on 'Children, Schools and Families' in their report on Assessment and Testing argued that the national standard attainment target tests have distorted the education of millions of children and have meant that children are fed a limited educational diet focused on getting them through the tests rather than improving their knowledge and understanding (House of Commons 2008). Moreover, the Chief Inspector of Schools has also spotted that focusing on exam-passing and teaching to the test rather than developing pupils' wider skills and knowledge was becoming increasingly widespread (Marley 2008b). A recent study by the Chartered Institute of Educational Assessors of 2,000 adults found that the majority did not believe that school exams reflected their true ability or predicted their future success or measured their real intelligence. It pointed out that pupils in England sit an average of 70 formal examinations, more than their international counterparts. Yet 60% of teachers who responded to a separate poll online said they did not think that exams were the best indicator of a pupil's ability and were not reflective of their future success in a job. Most of the adults responding to the former poll (62%) said that the feeling they most associated with an exam was 'butterflies in the stomach' but more extreme reactions included headaches, insomnia and vomiting. Just three out of ten associated exams with a 'sense of pride' (Davies 2008).

Meanwhile, the harmful effects of over-testing continue. A study based on 700 in-depth interviews with primary school children in England, for example, found that national tests on which school league tables are based left most children stressed (Curtis 2007b). In Japan forty schools were put on suicide watch and others on high alert after the death of headteachers and pupils caused by exam pressure and bullying. Two head teachers killed themselves when their schools were exposed as one of the many thousands that had been pretending to teach compulsory subjects but in fact skipped them in order to focus on cramming for the important university entrance exam (Fitzgerald 2006).

John Holt in *How Children Fail* argued that one of the things that children learn in school is how to cheat. He noted that that the pressure for high test scores created

"...a kind of cheating; teachers are not supposed to

cram children for these tests, but most of them do, particularly in schools that make a fetish of high test scores – which they call 'high standards' "(1964:153).

Indeed, in a system that now makes a fetish of test scores, one interesting and negative by-product of the pressures of the test culture is a recorded rise in actual cheating both by pupils and by teachers. Thus the headlines in the educational press such as 'Sharp rise in exam cheats', 'Explosion in cheating blamed on test culture' and 'Report reveals rise of cheats' (*Times Educational Supplement* 15/4/2005; 19/5/2006; 1/9/2006).

Interestingly, neuroscience seems to be proving the 1960s and 1970s writers correct in their critique of exams as anathema to real learning and harmful to feeling at ease in school. Bruno della-Chiesa, senior analyst in charge of the learning sciences and brain research project being run by the Organisation of Economic Cooperation and Development has said:

"Take exams. They are a completely useless way of ensuring that a child develops a skill. The exam system is not at all brain friendly. It doesn't take into account the way the brain works. Yet in every education system I know, the exams dictate how the system, the teachers and the students work".

He added that in some countries there was a desire to go back to the 1950s when teachers frightened children, but that when a child is scared the part of the brain that routes short-term memories to the cortex for thinking and longer term memory simply shuts down. So if neuroscientists were designing an education system fear and cramming would go and in their place would be fun, approval and recognition (Northern 2005).

Teacher Education

A further criticism levelled by the writers reviewed in

this book was that, far from challenging the authoritarian and reproductive nature of schooling, teacher education tends to reinforce and contribute to the problems. It has been said that teacher education has been characterised by the 'myth of the liberal college' – that is the myth that there is a contradiction between the liberal, progressive and democratic college or university on the one hand and the traditional, conservative and authoritarian school on the other (Bartholemew 1976). This myth suggests that student teachers are exposed to the more radical, democratic forms of teaching and learning during their courses in higher education with a high emphasis on pupil participation but are rapidly re-socialised into more authoritarian understandings and practices during their teaching practice and their subsequent employment in education. However, rather than there being a contradiction between the two, in terms of power over what is taught and learned, how and when, let alone the contradiction between 'do as I say' and 'do as I do' – in reality teacher education is often an authoritarian preparation for teaching in schools.

In regions such as Europe, America, Australia and New Zealand it has been argued that in recent decades teacher education has been subject to the increasing influence of both a neo-conservative ideology of control and a neo-liberal ideology of competition and accountability. The result is a combination of markets, standardisation, regulation and measurable outcomes. This, it is argued, has led to a situation of 'uniformity, conformity and compliance' and the prescription of alignment, consensus and consistency through bureaucratic and authoritarian control, a position *"which is antithetical to democratic participation"* (Delandshere and Petrosky 2004:126,133 but see also Apple 2001; Cochran Smith 2001; Griffiths 2000 and Hartley 2000). However, I would suggest that, while these changes may well have led to a further tightening of authoritarian practices in teacher education, in the main it has largely ever been thus. Indeed, I would also suggest that a global literature review of curriculum, teaching methodology and the scope of student decision-making inside teacher education would reveal a similar situation to that within schools, though on the whole without the element of force and violence that is often present in schools and which will be further discussed below.

In an earlier publication on Africa I described teacher education as an 'unvirtuous circle of authoritarian reproduction' (Harber 1997:93). While there have been some attempts to introduce more democratic methods into teacher education in at least one small part of Africa (Schweisfurth 2002), elsewhere not much seems to have changed. 'The Multi-Site Teacher Education Research Project' published three case studies from Africa in 2003. The one on Ghana said:

"Both student teachers and newly qualified teachers stressed that the most commonly used instructional approach in college was 'lectures with tutors dictating notes'. Rarely, it appears, were opportunities created for more interactive 'small group' work or discussions that would place much of the responsibility for developing personalised understanding of teaching on trainees"(Akyeampong 2003:viii).

In teacher education in Malawi

"Much learning is undertaken in a transmission style where information is projected with few opportunities for students to engage in debate and reflection. Questions were often informational and recall-based and much of the teaching appeared examination-driven, rarely departing from material likely to be found in assessment tasks. Few attempts seem to be made to capitalise on trainee insights into teaching and learning based on their experience in schools" (Kunje, Lewin and Stuart 2003:xiii).

While in Lesotho:

"Classroom observation confirmed the conservative nature of the programme in that, in practice, most teaching at the College is transmission-oriented, and there is little emphasis on independent learning, critical analysis, creative thought or learning to exercise professional judgement. The interaction between students and tutors during lectures involves a question-answer approach but questions are restrictive and do not allow for full independent thinking for students" (Lefoka and Sebatane 2003:x).

At the other end of the UN's *Human Development Index*, a study in Finland, a country at the top of recent international league tables for pupil achievement, found teacher education does not seem to provide student teachers with a sufficient experience of active, participatory learning methods. Teacher educators were said by former students to be dominating, unjust and authoritarian and the author concluded that there is a mutually reinforcing process of passivity between the cultures of teacher education and schools (Niemi 2002).

Chapter sixteen

Schooling Today:
Making Matters Worse?

"Schooling worldwide is characterised by misery, boredom, bullying, deceit, anxiety, humiliation, brutalisation, ethnic – and many other types of – discrimination, religious – and many other forms of – indoctrination, sexual – and many other kinds of – exploitation, and testing to destruction. It should not be like that. It should be fun" (Douse 2005:1).

A survey by the Howard League for Penal Reform of more than 3,000 children (in Britain) found that almost three-quarters had been assaulted over the previous year, and that two-thirds had been victims of theft. More than half had seen their property deliberately damaged, while others reported threats or verbal abuse. The study entitled *Children as Victims: Child-sized Crimes in a Child-Sized World,* found the majority of incidents occurred in schools and playgrounds, with much of the rest being between school and home. But children were unlikely to report the incident to police or teachers because they felt those adults would not be interested. Frances Crook, Director of the Howard League, said,*"Ironically, the very institutions where children should feel safest – their school environments set up and patrolled by adults – are where children are most commonly victimised"* (Ward 2007).

The critiques of schooling and teacher education put forward in the works of the authors reviewed earlier in this book still ring true in the light of the evidence discussed in the previous section. However, it is increasingly obvious that matters are considerably *worse* than the situations described in these key texts from the 1960s and 1970s.

Given the enormous global expenditure on schooling and the efforts towards education for all (largely interpreted as schooling), it should be unequivocally clear that schooling is consistently and unquestionably good for pupils and their societies. Despite the dominant global assumption and discourse that this is indeed the case, unfortunately it is far from uniformly being true. While schools do undoubtedly make a contribution to both individual and social development, the above critiques and supporting contemporary evidence show that this is despite their negative characteristics and comes at a heavy price for many of those concerned in terms of both their experiences in school and their life chances afterwards.

But matters are considerably worse as there is also mounting and very disturbing evidence of the violently harmful effects of schooling both on pupils and wider societies. The situation is worse both because more and more evidence is accumulating about what actually happens in schools and because globally more children and young people are in schools than they were thirty or forty years ago. Paradoxically, the more we have broken the taboos about gathering evidence and discussing violence in and by schools, the more global effort there has been to get the young into them. As Paulo Segio Pinheiro, the UN independent expert on violence against children put it, *"For a long time we only discussed access to education. But now we realise that access to education has to consider the issue of violence as well"* (cited in Global AIDS Alliance 2007:1).

Before examining some of the ways in which contemporary schooling is harmful to pupils, it is important to remember that no education is neutral. It can be used positively or negatively depending on the goals and priorities that are set and what is both encouraged or ignored. Or, as Josef Stalin put it, *"Education is a weapon, whose effects depend on who holds it in his hand and at whom it is aimed"* (quoted in Meighan 1994:4). He should know. Stalin went to school at a religious seminary in Tbilisi, the capital of Georgia and, as one historian stated, *"From the tyrannical priests he learnt exactly the tactics - surveillance, spying, invasion of inner life, violation of feelings, in Stalin's own words – that he would recreate in his Soviet police state"* (Montefiore 2007). It is perhaps also salutary to remember that both Pol Pot of the Khmer Rouge in Cambodia and his chief torturer known as Comrade Deuch both of whom were responsible for some 40,000 deaths, were both former school teachers.

Indeed, there is now considerable evidence suggesting that terrorism is positively linked to education i.e. people willing to use violence to pursue political ends are *more* likely to come from the higher educated sections of society. Opinion polls carried out in the West Bank and Gaza strip, for example, suggest that the more educated sections of the population are *less* likely to support dialogue and peaceful coexistence with Israel and more likely to support armed attacks. Similarly, Hezbollah fighters and Palestinian suicide bombers tend to come from the more educated sections of the Palestinian population. The same piece of research also found that violent Israeli extremists were also disproportionately from well-educated, high paid occupations, including teachers (Krueger and Maleckova 2003). Closer to home, it is well to remember that those convicted of the bomb attack at Glasgow airport in 2007 were highly educated medical doctors. In another paper discussing similar findings, Claude Berrebi of Princeton University comes to the important following conclusion:

"Policy makers, when trying to reduce terrorism via education or income, should focus not on the amount of education but on the content of education; changing the substance when needed in order to create positive stimulations towards democracy,

moderation, appeasement and coexistence. Not all education is equal, and as Martin Luther King once said in another context, 'education which stops with efficiency may prove the greatest menace to society. The most dangerous criminal may be the man gifted with reason but with no morals' " (Berrebi 2003:38).

In terms of the moral context of schooling, the United Nations has set out a very clear sense of purpose and guiding principles in the 1989 UN 'Convention on the Rights of the Child', signed by every country in the world except America and Somalia. For example:

"State Parties shall assure to the child who is capable of forming his or her own views the right to express those views freely in all matters affecting the child, the views of the child being given due weight in accordance with the age and maturity of the child"(Article 12).

"State Parties shall take all appropriate legislative, administrative, social and educational measures to protect the child from all forms of physical...violence, injury or abuse...while in the care of parent(s)...or any other person who has the care of the child" (Article 19).

However, as Nelson Mandela put it:

"Safety and security don't just happen: they are the result of collective consensus and public investment. We owe our children – the most vulnerable citizens in any society – a life free from violence and fear" (cited in PLAN (The Global Campaign to End Violence in Schools), Woking: PLAN, 2008: 3).

We now turn to the question of whether schools always live up to these principles both in terms of their role in reproducing violence and actively perpetrating it.

Bullying

Despite enormous global efforts to get more children into school, including fining and sending parents to jail in England, schools fail to protect children once they are there. Indeed, just walking through the door can pose a threat. School buildings themselves can be unsafe with dangers ranging from unhygienic toilets on the one hand, to buildings in danger of falling down, and failure to protect from earthquakes and fires on the other (Harber 2004:46). In July 2004, for example, a fire engulfed a primary school in Kumbhakonam in southern India, killing 78 children, some of whom had been left unsupervised. School buildings in the town do not require clearance from the fire department and even when the fire safety regulations are mandatory they are rarely observed. There are no trade standards for who can become an electrician and shoddy electrical equipment adds to the problem. All 23 of the school's teachers were reported as having run away from the school building as the fire spread, leaving the children behind. Some pupils who died were trapped because teachers had not unlocked an iron-grille door on the narrow staircase of the school building. Krishna Kumar of Delhi University's Department of Education said:

"It's chaotic. No norms and guidelines are followed anywhere in India when schools are established...A large number of schools, both private and government-run, are housed in very dangerous buildings, but issues such as fire safety are too sophisticated for government officials to enforce" (Rahman 2004 a and b).

But one significant threat to pupils whether or not the school buildings are safe is bullying. Bullying can take many forms – physical violence, threats, name-calling, sarcasm, spreading rumours, persistent teasing, exclusion from a group, tormenting, ridicule, humiliation and abusive comments. It has been known to be a serious problem in schools in many countries for many years but little seems to change (Roland and Munthe 1989; Oshako 1997; Ruiz 1998). One study of 13-year-olds in 27 countries found that the majority had been engaged in bullying at least some of the time (WHO 2002:29-30).

A summary of research on bullying in developing countries between 2003 and 2005 found that between one fifth and two thirds of children reported being bullied in the previous 30 days. The same report found that the picture was similar in OECD countries. Almost a quarter of seven million students questioned in Spain and a third of those surveyed in Australia reported being bullied by classmates. The report goes on to summarise research findings from Africa, Latin America and the Caribbean and Asia, all with depressingly high levels of bullying in schools:

"Yet despite the scale of the problem, only five of the countries examined in this report – Korea, Norway, Sri Lanka, the UK and the US – have laws explicitly prohibiting bullying in schools".

The report also points out that reducing or eliminating bullying is more difficult because many teachers and parents view bullying as an inevitable part of school life and growing up, though this is not necessarily the case. The report details the consequences of bullying, loss of self-esteem, shame, anxiety, truancy, concentration problems, reactive aggression, stress and serious psychological problems and even suicide. The bullies themselves also suffer from anxiety and depression and are at a higher risk of suicide and self-harm as well getting involved in criminal activity (PLAN 2008:36-41).

Pupils certainly seem to be afraid of bullying. A study of fear of becoming a victim of school violence based on the percentage of pupils across 33 countries who thought another student might hurt them at least once during the previous month found that on average 25.8% thought they might do so. There was no country where almost all pupils feel safe to learn at school (Akiba 2008).

A survey of 2,772 pupils in Britain in 2000 reported that more than half the respondents had experienced bullying but just under half said their school did not have an anti-bullying policy, despite being required to do so since 1999. Of those with a policy only about half said they thought it was working. Commenting on the findings the authors note that during their research heads told them that if you make a big thing out of bullying, parents will think you have a bullying problem in your school (Katz, Buchanan and Bream 2001:Ch.5). This was confirmed by the education select committee of the House of Commons in 2007 which thought that the problem of bullying was being played down to protect the reputations of schools. The same report quoted the telephone counselling sevice 'Childline' as having received 37,000 calls about bullying in 2005-6, up 12% on the previous year (Meikle 2007). In 2005 a poll of 500 children suggested that only 27% of 15-19 year-olds thought schools were doing enough to tackle the issue (*Times Educational Supplement* 18/11). In the same year the newly appointed Children's Commissioner for England said, "*I have had hundreds of conversations with children since accepting this post and I can tell you that the one thing every child I have met has been affected by, with virtually no exceptions, is bullying*" (Hill and Hinsliff 2005). In 2007 the UK came bottom of a league of 21 economically advanced countries put together by UNICEF on the well-being of children and adolescents. 35.8% of UK children reported being bullied in the last two months (Bosely 2007). A survey of 110,000 ten-to fifteen-year-olds by OFSTED found that 30% "*had been bullied a couple of times in the last four weeks*" (Marley 2007). Furthermore, both in and outside school, it has also been argued that web-based and mobile technologies now provide young people with 'an arsenal of weapons for social cruelty' (Shariff 2008).

Homophobic bullying is also a serious problem in schools. The Lesbian and Gay Association spoke to 750 lesbian, gay, bisexual and transgendered young people from 37 European countries and found that one in six had experienced discimination and prejudice at school (PLAN 2008:38-9). A survey of 877 13-15 year-olds and their teachers in Britain found that two thirds of the young people and three quarters of the teachers said they had seen homophobic bullying, but only 13% of the pupils knew of rules or policies to prevent or punish it. While a quarter of the pupils had been homophobically bullied, only 20% had reported it to a teacher. The then schools minister, Stephen Twigg, launched an anti-bullying week when he discovered that only 6% of schools had policies and procedures to deal with homophobic bullying of pupils or teachers (Richardson 2004). A survey of 1,145 gay teenagers in 2007 found that one in five had faced death threats from classmates whereas half of the teachers failed to act on homophobic language and bullying even when it occurred right in front of them (Bloom 2007). The gay rights group 'Stonewall' have stated that three quarters of lesbian, gay and bisexual adults have said that they regularly missed school because of harassment and half said they contemplated self-harm or suicide. 60% of lesbian and gay adults said they had been physically attacked at school and 82% of teachers said they were aware of homophobic bullying in schools (Taylor 2005). Meyer (2006) provides evidence of widespread homophobic bullying in America and a lack of intervention from educationalists to stop it with the result that "...*this teaches students that schools as institutions and their home communities, condone it*" (p.44). She argues that American schools generally place higher value on strength, competitiveness, aggressiveness and being tough – qualities widely seen as masculine. On the other hand, being creative, caring, good at school and quiet are often considered feminine qualities and are viewed by many as signs of weakness – particularly in boys, thereby leaving them open to homophobic bullying.

The inclusion of young people with special educational needs into mainstream schooling and away from special schools is an international policy issue in education. Yet this will only work if mainstream schools (or special schools for that matter) and the children in them act in a genuinely inclusive manner. Yet, disabled children are also more likely to be the targets of bullying and may be more willing to put up with abuse in order to gain access to social groups (Moore, Jones and Broadbent 2008). One study put it that:

"Having a disability or special educational needs is another risk factor for being a victim. Children with special educational needs are 2 to 3 times more at risk of being bullied; they are also more at risk of taking part in bullying others" (Smith and Ananiadou 2003:192).

In a sample of 101 boys and girls with statements of special educational needs for moderate learning difficulties in both special and mainstream school, 83% had experienced some form of bullying, whether verbal or physical. There were no significant differences between types of school, but about half the pupils reported that this bullying was related to their learning difficulties (Norwich and Kelly 2004). What both groups of young people have in common is their forced presence in a school, whether special or mainstream.

Bullying is also not confined to boys. Girl to girl bullying is an increasing problem and tends to be verbal, based on sexual insults and about competition for boys. Apart from the distress and unhappiness caused, the result can be absenteeism and some victims will move school to escape the problem (Bloom 2009; Duncan 1996 and 2006).

While it is known that bullying in schools exists and is widespread, it is usually assumed that bullying results from faults in the character of the children in school. However, a review by Smith (2005) revealed that despite many years of expensive research and intervention, bullying had not been reduced much at all. This might well be because it is the school organisation and culture itself that is conducive to bullying:

"Imagine being made by law to attend an institution six hours a day, five days a week where you were controlled in everything you do, for no pay nor worthwhile outcomes for you personally. Imagine you were so controlled in this environment that you were punished for speaking without permission, for not sitting in a particular position, for laughing out loud, for whispering. Imagine being told to do things you had no interest in, and then being harassed for not doing it as well as that person thinks you can. Imagine your ability or performance being constantly measured and compared against your peers. Imagine being told what to wear down to the tiniest detail, being forbidden expressions of personality such as jewellery or make-up. Imagine being forced to cut or grow your hair until it met with someone else's approval. Imagine being so controlled in every way that even your bodily functions are at someone else's discretion and you need permission to eat, drink or go to the toilet" (Duncan 2007a).

As Duncan points out, given the oppressive ethos, it is a wonder there is not more trouble in schools. However, the ethos of schooling is also essentially competitive, with winners and losers and when people are both losers and bossed around in a situation they cannot change and where they daily witness double standards in the behaviour expected of them and those in authority, they take out their frustration and anger on the only targets available – their weaker peers. However, the good news is that bullying rates do differ between individual schools and there is much that can be done. The policies and ethos of schools regarding inclusivity and meeting individual needs can genuinely reduce bullying (Duncan 2007b). However, it first has to be recognised that the problem is not necessarily with individual pupils and, as we have seen from the evidence on bullying presented above, this institutional analysis is not yet sufficiently accepted and acted upon.

Indeed, there are parallels between discussion of bullying and arguments over the phenomenon of school shootings in America, such as the much-publicised case of Columbine High in 1999. One piece of research, for example, concentrates on the personal characteristics of the shooters – that they are shy, have been shunned by their classmates, lacked empathy, were social isolates, had a low level of tolerance of frustration and had been bullied (www.research.iu.edu/news/stories/0128.html).

Essentially, from this point of view, the problem starts and is located with the individuals concerned. However, others argue that the phenomenon of rampage school shootings in American schools is not just a problem of the activities of individual pupils, however socially isolated, but essentially results from the organisational failings of schools. In each case the pupils had a troubled history, including bullying, but the schools failed to act upon their own records because information in the schools was fragmented due to the segregation of tasks and an ambivalence about the key purposes of the school. As a result of this ambivalence, traditional academic concerns win out as a priority over emotional and social development, both teachers and counsellors are not properly trained to identify and deal with personal problems and there is a dearth of resources devoted to such concerns. The pupils who eventually went on to shoot fellow pupils and teachers were not disruptive and so were not noticed:

"In loosely coupled systems like schools, we argue, serious personal problems are allowed to fester because they do not impede the dominant organisational goals: order and minimum academic standards. Our study of Heath and Westside suggest that school shooters go unnoticed because many are not behaving in ways that interrupt the functioning of their schools and hence their behaviour is not interpreted as indicative of a potential for violent behaviour or of social and emotional problems" (Fox and Harding 2005:82).

The authors of this article also point out that at Columbine there were reports that the shooters had been viciously humiliated by their peers in the presence of their teachers, who failed to intervene on their behalf. Also in a number of other cases it was reported that individual members of the school staff were aware that the shooters were being bullied or humiliated but did little to end the abuse. The conclusion is that these shootings did not happen by accident or on a completely random basis but were the result of interplay between the priorities of the cultural environment in which the schools operate, the organisational structure of the school and the routine cognitive practices of its staff.

But teachers can also be guilty of more direct forms of bullying. Interviews carried out with 40 first year university students in Russia found that teachers had called pupils a wide range of insulting words if they did not learn fast enough; used their classroom pointers as tools of punishment and intimidation; destroyed school accessories if they did not comply with school regulations; threw various objects at pupils and physically attacked them by hitting their heads, pushing them or banging their heads against the blackboard (Zdravomyslova and Gorshkova 2006). A study of violence in The Free State of South Africa found that the sample of 800 teachers reported that 43% of educators in their school had threatened one or more learners in their school over the period of a year, whereas 17% had attacked or assaulted one or more learners in their school during the same period (de Wet 2007). A study of stress among 271 pupils in Poland found that an important factor was teachers' verbal abuse of children (Piekarska 2000). In sub-Saharan Africa research suggests that female teachers often call on male teachers to carry out corporal punishment while they themselves resort to emotional abuse and insulting language to control students (PLAN 2008:13). In America a study of fifty students at alternative schools found that 86% reported at least one incident of adult physical maltreatment and 88% reported at least one incident of adult psychological maltreatment while they were in mainstream schools. Almost twice as many students reported that an adult rather than a peer was involved in their worst school experience. The authors commented that, *"these findings indicate that students are being bullied by teachers to a surprising degree and in a wide range of destructive and harmful ways"* (Whitted and Dupper 2008). Corporal punishment in schools, another form of bullying by teachers, is discussed in more detail below.

Corporal Punishment

"Teachers always hold a stick. Once I argued with a teacher. I was instructed to lean against the wall and I was hit three times by a stick. I was so stressed out and I perspired heavily" (Quotation from young person in Thailand in PLAN 2008:11).

A form of violence institutionally sanctioned in many schools around the world, and strongly criticised in the books reviewed in the first part of this book, is corporal punishment. In 90 countries out of 197 monitored by the *Global Initiative to End All Corporal*

Punishment of Children, corporal punishment remains legal despite consistent and overwhelming evidence of its harmful effects and it being incompatible with the United Nations Convention on the Rights of the Child. In the developed or industrialised world, it is still legal in France, Korea and a number of Australian and American states (PLAN 2008:12,14). In other countries where it has been officially banned, such as South Africa, (Nelson Mandela Foundation 2005) and China (PLAN 2008:12) it is still widely used, suggesting that corporal punishment in school still exists in at least one third and perhaps as much as half of the countries of the world. Britain only finally legally banned corporal punishment from all schools in 1999 but even then a survey of 1,000 parents in England and Wales in 2000, found that 51% thought that corporal punishment should be reintroduced in schools (Carvel 2000). A similar poll in 2008 found that 44% of parents would like to see corporal punishment reinstated in schools (TES 11/1/2008). Further examples of contexts where corporal punishment is still in use can be found in Harber,2004:Ch.5 and PLAN 2008: 11-19).

While there has been a drop in the number of countries officially using corporal punishment since the 1960s, in some ways the situation is worse because the practice remains common globally despite widespread debate, all that is known about its harmful effects and the existence of many positive alternatives. Indeed, in June 2006 the UN Committee on the Rights of the Child adopted General Comment No.8 on: *"The right of the child to protection from corporal punishment and other cruel or degrading forms of punishment".*

So while there is no evidence that corporal punishment improves behaviour or academic achievement – quite the opposite (PLAN 2008) – there is considerable evidence of its harmful effects, including physical harm and even death. For example, corporal punishment was outlawed in Uganda recently but only after one incident where five students were admitted into hospital with severe head injuries after being assaulted by their teachers. The students had failed to report a fight between two other students and so the teachers decided to punish the entire dormitory. Two weeks before this a 20-year-old female student received severe back injuries after a beating by her geography teacher for failing to complete an assignment. She was also admitted to hospital and could not walk unaided (Kigotho 2006).

The World Health Organisation, which explicitly includes corporal punishment in school as part of child abuse, states that:

"Importantly there is now evidence that major adult forms of illness – including ischaemic heart disease, cancer, chronic lung disease, irritable bowl syndrome and fibromyalgia – are related to experiences of abuse during childhood. The apparent mechanism to explain these results is the adoption of behavioural risk factors such as smoking, alcohol abuse, poor diet and lack of exercise...Similarly there are many studies demonstrating short-term and long-term psychological damage. Some children have a few symptoms that do not reach clinical levels of concern, or else are at clinical levels but not as high as in children generally seen in clinical settings. Other survivors have serious psychiatric symptoms, such as depression, anxiety, substance abuse, aggression, shame or cognitive impairments. Finally, some children meet the full criteria for psychiatric illnesses that include post-traumatic stress disorder, major depression, anxiety disorders and sleep disorders" (WHO 2002:69/70).

In Britain, one historian has concluded that what corporal punishment taught children was not discipline, but dislike of teachers, anger and a need for revenge (Middleton 2008). Not surprisingly, elsewhere corporal punishment also rarely makes pupils feel enthusiastic about schooling or learning. In Nepal corporal punishment is an important reason for school drop out (Teeka-Bhattarai 2006), while in Botswana:

"The more obvious effects of corporal punishment included increased student anxiety, fear or resentment in class. Girls, in particular, remained silent, and were mistakenly dubbed as 'lazy' or 'shy' by some teachers, and so did some boys. Other boys absconded or refused to cooperate in female teachers' classes...Other studies have also found that excessive physical punishment, generally of boys, can prompt truancy" (Humphreys 2006).

Nevertheless, historically, authority and order in schools has consistently been associated with violent imposition:

"From their inception, formal schools in Western capitalist societies have been designed to discipline bodies as well as to regulate minds. A key purpose of modern state schooling has been the formation and conduct of beliefs, as well as the acquisition of prescribed knowledge. School discipline has frequently been overt and physically violent, with students most often the target of teacher-administered punishment" (Rousmaniere, Dehli and Ning de Coninck-Smith 1997:3).

A major factor in its global spread was colonialism, particularly British colonialism. In Africa, for example, it has been argued that although corporal punishment is now sometimes justified on the grounds that it is 'part of African culture', evidence on pre-colonial education systems suggests that this is unlikely. As Tafa argues in relation to pre-colonial Botswana, where corporal punishment is still widely used in schools, *"there is no evidence to suggest that children were flogged every step of the way"* (2002:23). He notes that when neighbouring Zambia banned caning in 2000 it was described as 'a brutal relic of British rule'. He argues that

"Caning became ingrained in the popular minds as critical to school discipline hence the common refrain that its abolition equals classroom disorder and failure. The result is a cycle of caning transmitted from one generation to another and justified on the basis of experience and sentiment...In a class of 35-40 authoritarianism is a means of orchestrating 'mob control'. Instant punishment and military style parades typical of Botswana schools are all about social control. Teachers are saddled with systemic constraints of large and mixed class sizes for which no extra resources were made available" (Tafa 2002:23).

Sometimes even the teachers themselves are caned. The Tanzania Teachers' Union took legal action when 19 primary school teachers were caned by a police officer after poor examination results and staff lateness at three schools. The teachers were, understandably, angry and 'ashamed to meet my pupils now' at their treatment but there was no mention of whether they themselves meted out similar treatment to the pupils in their schools (news.bbc.co.uk/2/hi/Africa/7889141.stm).

Sexual Harassment and Violence

One way in which schools are now clearly worse than previously thought is in relation to sexual harassment and violence. It is not so much that the situation has got worse but we know more about what goes on and it is becoming increasingly unacceptable, if still a major problem:

"The number of children across the world subjected to sexual abuse is shocking. 'The World Health Organisation' estimated in 2002 that 150 million girls and 73 million boys under the age of 18 had been raped or suffered other forms of sexual abuse" (PLAN 2008:22).

Of course, as PLAN also point out, completely reliable and accurate figures of how much of this takes place in and around schools are difficult to come by because of the shame of the victims, lack of certainty that reporting will lead to action against the perpetrator and, it must be added, cover-up and silences among the perpetrators. However, it is possible to gauge the extent of the problem and to conclude that it is serious.

In 2004 I published a substantial chapter on this issue and the detrimental effects it has on female learners but the problem certainly does not seem to have been solved or gone away. In 2008, for example, Amnesty International published a report tellingly entitled *Safe Schools: Every Girl's Right.* In the introduction it states:

"Every day, girls face being assaulted on their way to school, pushed and hit in school grounds, teased and insulted by their classmates, and humiliated by having rumours circulated about them through whisper campaigns, mobile phones or the internet. Some are threatened with sexual assault by other students, offered higher marks by teachers for sexual favours, even raped in the staff room. Some are beaten or caned in the name of school discipline...Violence against girls takes place in and around many educational institutions all over the world. It is inflicted not only by teachers, but also by administrators, other school employees, fellow students and outsiders. The result is that countless girls are kept out of school, drop out of school, or do not participate fully in school" (2008:1/2).

As the report points out, there is an increased risk of violence if the girl is lesbian or disabled. The report quotes evidence from the USA, Malawi, Zimbabwe, Bangladesh, India, Nepal, Pakistan, Sri Lanka and Latin America on high levels of sexual harassment in schools. In Togo it is so common that an entire vocabulary has evolved to describe it. One US-based organisation dedicated to the prevention of school violence found that in just 10 days in early 2007 18 cases of sexual assault occurred in US schools (p.18,29,31).

As the Amnesty International report argued, acknowledging that there is a problem and that it is causing harm is the first step along the way to solving it. Yet the Global AIDS Alliance (2007) reviewed the Educational Sector Plans of ten African countries that are being supported by the *Education for All – Fast Track Initiative,* none of which outlines a comprehensive intervention package to prevent, counter and respond to school-related violence. However, "...*recent studies in Africa demonstrate that between 16 and 47 per cent of girls in primary or secondary school report sexual abuse or harassment from male teachers or classmates*" (2007:3). They are also critical (p.13) of two major aid donors, the United States Agency for International Development (USAID) and the British Department for International Development (DfID), for falling short of what is needed to ensure that schools are safe learning environments for the world's children, including girls. Research for the British Department for International Development in Ghana and Botswana also found bullying, sexual harassment and aggressive behaviour by boy students against girls in schools, and that such behaviour is rarely punished as teachers regard such acts as normal and a 'natural' part of growing up (id21 2005). UNESCO's '*Education For All Global Monitoring Report*' (2008) also recognises that sexual harassment and sexual violence are a major problem, citing the UN's own report on violence against children (Pinheiro 2006) as to the widespread nature of the problem.

PLAN (2008:22-33) cites evidence of significantly high levels of sexual violence against girls by students and staff in Uganda, South Africa, Zambia, Botswana,

Ghana, Malawi, Zimbabwe, Ecuador, the Dominican Republic, Honduras, Guatemala, Mexico, Nicaragua, Panama, Thailand and Nepal. However, the phenomenon is not only located in developing countries. For example, a study in the Netherlands showed that 27% of students reported being sexually harassed by school personnel. In Sweden researchers found that among 17- and 18-year-olds 49% felt that sexual harassment at school was a significant problem. In France 3.3% of *all* sexual attacks take place within the school environment. Evidence that this is a worrying issue that occurs at unacceptable levels is also cited from Switzerland, Spain, Germany, Belgium and Canada. In Britain Ministers ordered urgent action to tackle sexual bullying and harassment in the classroom (*The Guardian* 6/12/2008), while the Chief Executive of the General Teaching Council said that it was preparing itself for *"an upsurge in the number of teachers being publicly accused of unacceptable sexual conduct"* (*Times Educational Supplement* 7/9/2007). Of course, sexual harassment and abuse in schools can also be homosexual as well as heterosexual (O'Moore and Minton 2003; Jones 1994; Williams 2005).

In my book *Schooling As Violence* (2004:Ch.7) I noted that there seems to be a particular problem in South Africa and why this might be the case. One statistic really stood out. A Medical Research Council survey carried out in 1998 found that among those rape victims who specified their relationship to the perpetrator, 37.7% said their schoolteacher or principal had raped them (Human Rights Watch 2001:42). As someone very familiar with South Africa, it took some time for this figure to sink in even with me. Section V of the report details many actual cases of sexual abuse carried out by teachers in schools. The situation does not seem to have improved. Twenty-seven complaints of sexual misconduct against teachers were received by the South African Council of Educators between January and October 2008 and in some cases the teacher-pupil relationships took place with the consent of the children's parents based on some kind of financial agreement. The Chief Executive Officer of the Council said,

"It has been very disturbing that there have been cases where students have been minors. Children as young as nine have been found to be involved with teachers. There have also been cases of impregnation. Council finds that completely intolerable. While girl learners are abused by other members of society, we definitely have jurisdiction over teachers. The age of learners, their consent, parental consent or their location in a different school will not mitigate the culpability of a teacher in this regard" (Mail and Guardian Online 8/12/2008).

The main cause of sexual harassment and violence in schools is that traditional gender stereotypes and unequal power relationships are not challenged but reproduced by the school. Moreover, the authoritarian, closed nature of much of schooling meshed with patriarchal values and behaviours provides a context in which the patterns of sexual harassment described above can happen. As the PLAN report says (2008:26):

"Girls in societies where women are accorded a lower or more passive status (and where practices such as infanticide, female genital cutting and honour killings take place) are more likely to suffer sexual violence at school".

The report also points out that unless teachers themselves have been educated about gender and power issues, they are likely to model behaviour that reflects their own experiences and those of the wider community. They go on to note that a South African survey found that 47% of female teachers in a pilot project had suffered physical abuse at the hands of an intimate partner, and 25% of male teachers admitted that they had been physically abusive to an intimate partner (PLAN 2008:26). A survey of South Africa and English teacher education students found that few had studied or discussed gender issues,including the nature of masculinity, either at school or in their teacher education (Harber and Serf 2006).

As I argued, elsewhere, the values and behaviours of different models of masculinity are socially learned, not genetically determined (2004:Ch.7) However, schools not only do not necessarily educate about masculinity in order to curb more violent interpretations of it but can also actually encourage them:

"Schools, clubs and colleges are institutions where gender is actively forged. Gender isn't just reflected or expressed. They are places where a certain type of 'top dog' masculinity is made, celebrated confirmed through daily acts of violence and bullying" (Salisbury and Jackson 1996:105).

In an analysis of *Cultural Capital and High School Bullies*, Klein (2006) argues that in order to build cultural capital in male peer hierarchies in schools, boys have to exhibit the hallmarks of normalised masculinity – hyper-masculine identification, athletics, fighting, distance from homosexuality, dominant relationships with girls, socio-economic status and disdain for academic study. She further argues through a study of twelve boys that the perpetrators of high school shootings between 1996 and 2002 in America were bullied and harassed because they lacked these characteristics and eventually responded by trying to prove their masculinity through resorting to overwhelming violence. She concludes that schools need to find a way to have a larger continuum of values activities to support a more diverse student body and not just accept dominant and violent forms of masculinity:

"Schools can convey values of community, support, cooperation and compassion...Today, however, faculty and parents often support values that spurn less masculine – seeming, less athletic, less typical boys. This is dangerous destructive, and in the wake of school shootings, unconscionable...schools and suburbs can become associated with prisons, where outcasts know no way out, and can hardly imagine life being different...School faculty also maintain these conditions through lack of appropriate intervention and prevention practices or sometimes through direct support of destructive cultural mores" (2006:66/7).

Race, Ethnicity and the 'Other'

"For years that was all I knew about the Hazaras, that they were Mogul descendants, and that they looked a little like Chinese people. School textbooks rarely mentioned them and referred to their ancestry in passing...Then I found one of my mother's old history books...I read that my people, the Pashtuns, had persecuted and oppressed the Hazaras...The book said that part of the reason Pashtuns had oppressed the Hazaras was that Pashtuns were Sunni Muslims, while Hazaras were Shi'a...The following week I showed the book to my teacher and pointed to the chapter on the Hazaras. He skimmed through a couple of pages, snickered, handed the book back. 'That's one thing Shi'a people do well', he said, picking up his papers, 'passing themselves off as martyrs'. He wrinkled his nose when he said the word Shi'a as if it were some kind of disease" (Khaled Hosseini *The Kite Runner* Bloomsbury Publishing 2003 p.8).

Schooling has always played a part, via socialisation and indoctrination, in the creation, reproduction, modification and vilification of group identities and stereotypes. Postman and Weingartner in their book *Teaching As a Subversive Activity* described above (ch.11), wrote that *"it is generally assumed that people of other tribes have been victimised by indoctrination from which our tribe has remained free"*. Brown (2005), for example, has argued that in Malaysia the government has sought to use schooling to remove tensions between nation-building and ethnicity through a didactic pedagogical approach to educational development which promotes a concept of nationhood that, rather than transcending ethnic allegiances, is explicitly based on ethnic stratification.

Two extreme and well-known negative examples of racial indoctrination and stereotyping in schools explicitly aimed at racial inequality and violence are Nazi Germany and Apartheid South Africa. There was plenty of historical warning from these examples and from the history of colonialism (see e.g. Mangan 1993) about the consequences of this type of racist education. But history, including the history of education, does have a habit of repeating mistakes and there are many contemporary examples where schooling has played a part in reproducing and perpetrating hatred of the 'other' through the content of school textbooks and the activities of teachers. In this sense schooling is again worse because in too many places - Bosnia Herzegovina, Kosovo, Cyprus, Palestine and Israel, eastern Germany, India, Pakistan and Rwanda - lessons from history have not been learnt and schooling has played a part in fermenting inter-communal violence. I have discussed the evidence for these countries in some detail elsewhere and described it as schools being involved in 'pro-racist' activities (Harber 2004:Ch.6). Further analysis of how governments in India and Pakistan have used school curricula and textbooks to create antagonism and hatred between the two national identities is provided in Lall (2008).

However, one of the most disturbing examples was Rwanda, where in the genocide of April 1994 when between 800,000 and a million people were murdered, Hutu teachers not only preached hatred of the Tutsi 'other' but were also actively involved in the killing:

"Neighbours hacked neighbours to death in their homes, and colleagues hacked colleagues to death in the workplaces. Doctors killed their patients and school teachers killed their pupils..." (Gourevitch 1998:114-5).

Yet, despite all the efforts of the post-genocide government, there are still reports that 'genocide ideology' can be found in the country's schools. Research in 32 schools by a committee of MPs found that ethnic hatred is still prevalent among pupils in most of them and manifests itself in graffiti and general harassment such as putting rubbish in the beds of genocide survivors, tearing their clothes, destroying their school books, mattresses and kitbags. In some schools teachers themselves were accused of sowing the seeds of hatred among the pupils. In one school, investigators found a teachers' report concluded *"Rwanda has made considerable progress in promoting co-existence between its people but there is obviously a long way to go. It took more than three decades to teach ethnic division in Rwanda. So it might take just as long to heal it"* (BBC News 24 19/2/2008).

Militarisation

"School is the army for kids. Adults make them go there, and when they get there, adults tell them what to do, bribe and threaten them into doing it, and punish them when they don't" (John Holt quoted in Meighan 1994:10).

Schools are not just like the military in the sense of compulsory attendance and authoritarianism, however, nor in the similar use of compulsory uniforms. While historically there is a strong connection between schooling and the need to create a loyal population ready to defend borders, the military, training how to kill, are actively present in schools globally (Harber 2004:Ch.9). This is despite centuries of violent conflict and all that we know about violence as having a sociological and educational basis rather than a biological one (UNESCO 1989). On this front as well, many schooling systems have not so much been slow learners as non-learners. In Poland, for example, and despite not having been at war for over 60 years, all 15- and 16-year-olds must take a war survival course, teaching them how to put on a gas mask, how to shoot a gun, how to throw a grenade, how to identify guns and army ranks and how to use bunkers. The author of the article describing this course comments:

"Still, current students might consider themselves lucky. Only 20 years ago, children had to learn how to march. I can remember as a schoolchild being assessed on my gas-mask skills. I mastered every move to perfection but I didn't get the top mark. When I asked the teacher why she marked me down, she said: 'You took a deep breath before putting on the mask. In a real situation you'd be dead by now' " (Kaczmarek 2008).

In Russia, the Mayor of Moscow signed a decree such that all 15- and 16-year-old boy school leavers will be sent on military training. The boys will tackle assault courses, drill with loaded Kalashnikovs and meet serving officers and soldiers in order to encourage a sense of patriotic responsibility. This followed on a law passed by the Russian parliament the year before that reintroduced mandatory military studies for all students in the final two years of secondary school (Holdsworth 2004).

In America, Saltman and Gabbard (2003:1/2) describe different forms of military training and experience in schools and argue that:

"These programs parallel the Boy Scouts and Girl Scouts by turning hierarchical organisation, competition, group cohesion and weaponry into fun and games".

In Britain, Gordon Brown and Ed Balls, the Prime Minister and Schools Minister at the time of writing, have supported plans for pupils in comprehensive schools to be given military drills and weapons training through the cadet corps. Such experiences are already disproportionately more common in independent and grammar schools. One of the ideas behind this is that it would bring more discipline and order (*The Observer* 6/4/2008; *The Independent* 15/5/2008 and 19/5/2008).

Of course, as many of these sources note and provide evidence for, all such military training in schools also gives a distinct market advantage to the military in terms of future recruitment. Another objection raised by some might concern the wisdom of teaching even more people, who may or may not eventually join a professional army, about how to use guns given global concern about rising levels of violence. However, in Texas, it is not the pupils that are armed – in the small town of Harrold teachers have been permitted to carry concealed guns in the classroom to protect against the sort of school killings in American schools discussed above. Others, including teacher unions, thought that arming teachers would make the situation more, not less, dangerous (*The Guardian* 18/8/2008).

In an interesting analysis of *Education for War in Israel*, Gor (2003) argues that children in Israel are psychologically prepared for war in a variety of ways:

"*The message transmitted through the teaching of holidays, literature, history and the Bible, even through ceremonies in schools is that power represents the only option that guarantees life. What is at stake is our physical survival; it is a question of the survival of the fittest. There is no alternative. One has to be strong, powerful and ready for war...On Independence Day, children are taught that Arabs wanted to throw us into the sea and that the armies of all seven Arab states surrounding us invaded*

Israel. Kids visit military camps and teachers display flags of various military corps...Boys are taught to admire the soldiers and identify with them; they are encouraged to develop fantasies of being fighter pilots, tank drivers or submarine commanders. Girls are encouraged to mail sweets to the front and wait for their hero soldiers to return from the army. They are expected to give unconditional support" (178-80).

Gor goes on to describe how children in kindergarten are dressed up in uniforms and marched around while singing patriotic songs and comments:

"The emotional imprinting at a very early age, prior to the development of critical faculties, makes it highly unlikely that, at later age, children will express doubts, ask questions or re-examine what has been drilled into them" (p.180).

The military exists, by definition, to be prepared to fight violent conflicts. It is highly debatable whether the kind of unquestioning authority exercised in the military is suitable for educating young people in a democratic society or whether schools should put emphasis on training to kill over and above peaceful conflict resolution and management.

Chapter seventeen

What is to be Done?

"When you take the free will out of education, that turns into schooling". And,

"It is a great triumph of compulsory government monopoly of mass schooling that among even the best of my fellow teachers, and among even the best of my students parents, only a small number can imagine a different way to do things" (John Taylor Gatto cited in Meighan 1994:3,6).

The problems with schooling seem so deep and intractable that sometimes it is difficult to be optimistic about the future. Indeed, little of a fundamental nature has changed in the last fifty years and in some ways matters now actually appear to be worse. This is not to say that trenchant critiques and alternative viewpoints and ideas on education do not exist and have not been aired – witness, for example, the output of *Educational Heretics Press* and *Education Now* since the 1980s. It is just that traditional, compulsory bureaucratic models of schooling as education are an entrenched, powerful and hegemonic orthodoxy in the minds of governments, parents and many within education itself. Current models of schooling are consistently portrayed in a taken-for-granted, common sense manner as the *only* way to organise education in the media, by governments, by international institutions, by many national and international NGO's and by most academics. They are seen as a given good and even serious crises cannot dent official faith in the traditional school as an inherently and solely beneficial institution. One article on children affected by HIV/AIDS brings this into stark relief on a global scale, arguing that even when faced with some sort of serious crisis or emergency international agencies such as the World Bank automatically see the solution as the educational status quo i.e. getting as many children as possible into

"traditional, formal schools and shoring up existing teaching and administrative cadres...The question of what types of schooling might better serve students has, however, for the most part been ignored..." (Kendall 2008:375,381).

The problem is, as the author notes, that existing notions of schooling and education are well-established and relatively comfortable for those in power.

If, on the whole, you share the critical views of schooling expressed by those who wrote the books summarised earlier, then it is easy to despair at the lack of progress and even the evidence of regression. Existing education systems for the majority seem permanently glued to current practices of curriculum, teaching and assessment which often damage learners and their societies. Nothing seems to shake the faith, partly because of the difficulty of questioning and shifting such overwhelmingly hegemonic ideas and partly because many of those with power, privilege and comfort have a vested interest in matters continuing as they are. However, and despite all the evidence to the contrary, something, some vestige of hope, must keep those of us who wish for fundamental change in education going. Perhaps the key to survival in the conflict over educational purposes and processes is lowered expectations, keeping hope in perspective and the celebration of small, localised victories when they occur. A kind of restricted and realistic optimism.

While the main aim of this book was to consider whether the critiques of some key writers on education from the 1960s and 1970s were still valid today (they are and even more so), it is important to try to end on a more positive note. This final, section of the book will therefore briefly do two things. First, it will set out some the key areas of concern about the current orthodoxy of bureaucratic schooling and suggest some sources that both provide a cogent critique of existing practices and suggest positive ways forward. Second, it will signpost some further sources of theoretical and practical relevance both to providing alternatives to current forms of schooling and reducing the damage done by schooling.

However, before this, an important initial point to make is, *first, do no harm*. When you are in a hole, stop digging. Before any sort of major or minor educational change in a positive direction it is, at the very least, vital to stop the direct forms of harm and violence inflicted on young people via schooling that have been described above. For example, while corporal punishment still exists in schools in many countries, there are active international campaigns to eradicate it and there is no doubt that its prevalence is declining. The January 2009 newsletter of 'The Global Initiative to End All Corporal Punishment for Children' notes that, on top of those countries already having banned corporal punishment,

"the year begins with 23 states having achieved law reform and governments in at least a further 24 committed to prohibition and/or actively considering draft legislation. Campaigns are now under way all over the world".

While the newsletter does also provide evidence on the continuing use of corporal punishment in schools it at least seems to be a slowly declining phenomenon in schools globally. Similarly, it is to be hoped that increasing international awareness and debates about sexual harassment and abuse in schools will, probably slowly but eventually, stop this practice in schools.

If some, or even much, of the bad can eventually be stopped, what then is the direction of change for good? One of the key criticisms of the writers of the 1960s and 1970s was that schools are essentially authoritarian institutions. This is inconsistent with the need to experience democracy in order to learn to be a democratic citizen. Democracy as a form of government has spread rapidly, if imperfectly and incompletely, since the 1960s and 1970s - a glance at a map of the world thirty or forty years ago would instantly show many more one party and military states than exist today. Democracy is now acknowledged as *the* goal of political development for all states by the United Nations. As the Nobel Prize winner Amartya Sen has argued (1999) democratic freedom is both development *in itself* and a better means of achieving social and economic progress than any of the alternatives. For Sen, and of significance to education, development as freedom consists of the expansion of the 'capabilities' of people to achieve 'substantial freedoms' that people themselves have reason to value rather than just regard as economically useful, such as happiness, desire-fulfilment or choice. And however imperfect democracies often are in practice, they at least enhance the frequency and possibility of settling disputes and conflicts peacefully, both internally and externally.

So, for this writer, the key overall goal of education should be the creation of democratic citizens disposed to the peaceful management of conflicts. However, as I have written before:

"Democracy is only sustainable in a supportive political culture where a sufficient proportion of the population have a high commitment to democratic values, skills and, particularly, behaviours. This is based on an understanding of democracy that goes beyond the minimum ritual of voting (or not voting) every four or five years in an election. While democracy does require an informed citizenry capable of making genuine political choices, it also requires a

fuller and deeper notion of democracy that forms the basis of a democratic society in which people actually behave in a democratic manner in their daily interactions. Democracy is not genetic, it is learned behaviour. There is nothing in our genes to programme us as democrats or dictators at birth. Therefore education must have a clear idea of the sort of democratic person it hopes to cultivate. What are the characteristics of such a person? Somebody described as democratic would, for example, celebrate social and political diversity, work for and practice mutual respect between individuals and groups, regard all people as having equal social and political rights as human beings, respect evidence in forming their own opinions and respect the opinions of others based on evidence, be open to changing one's mind in the light of new evidence and possess a critical and analytical stance towards information. The democratic citizen would possess a proclivity to reason, open-mindedness and fairness and the practice of cooperation, bargaining, compromise and accommodation" (Harber 2004:137).

If education, whether in something called a school or not, is to be consistent with this then there is a need to move away from the dominant, negative characteristics of formal schooling identified in the critiques of the selected educational writers from the 1960s and 1970s. First, educational institutions need to be more democratic in their decision-making structures with learners having a voice in how the institution is run, what is learned, when, where and how. Not only should this be a matter of principle in a democratic society, but there is also considerable evidence that it both helps to create more democratic citizens and enhance learning as measured by conventional means such as examinations and continuous assessment (Harber 2009a).

However, this does not sit well with a top-down, prescriptive, one size fits all national curriculum either in Britain or elsewhere. Indeed, Elliott (2007) argues that the educational implications of Sen's capability theory of democratic development, noted above, are close to the values expressed by John Dewey in his work *Education and Democracy* which, if put into practice, would result in a curriculum very different from the state-sponsored, directive curriculum with minimal student choice that is common in many countries today. Although there is a long curricular continuum in terms of the degree of potential learner involvement in decision-making, stretching from a completely blank sheet of paper where learners decide on their own curriculum at the one end to a more restricted notion of having some sort of subject choice and doing some projects at the other (Meighan 1988; Davies, Harber and Schweisfurth 2002:Ch.5), there is generally a need for much more personal choice and flexibility about what is learned, when where and how. This may well exist in a context where very broad learning outcomes in terms of the skills and values that are consistent with a democratic citizen are set by the government, but for many or most contemporary education systems there is a need to move in the direction of more personalised forms of educational provision where learners have a significant and controlling say over their own learning. Two recent books are helpful discussions of both the principles and practice of more personalised forms in enhancing the relevance, interest and usefulness of education to learners (Meighan 2005; Webster 2008) as is the website personalisededucationnow.org.uk.

In keeping with more democratic and personalised forms of education, the overwhelming tyranny of examinations and testing must also be eliminated or drastically reduced:

"To me, it seems clear that the greater threat posed by a test, the less it can measure, far less encourage learning. There are many reasons for this. One of the most obvious, and most important, is that whenever a

student knows that they are being judged by the results of a tests, they turn their attention from the material to the tester. What is paramount is not the course or its meaning to the student but whatever is in the tester's mind. Learning becomes less a search than a battle of wits. The tester, whoever they are, is no longer a helper, but an enemy" (Holt 1971:53).

The negative effects of over-testing have been known about for a long time. Dore (1976) and Oxenham (1984) both detailed on a global scale the way that tests and examinations distort the quality of the educational experience, encourage concentration on some parts of a curriculum at the expense of others, encourage a cramming of facts and create an overwhelming dependency on extrinsic goals, rather than intrinsic ones: *"In short, it encourages a wholly negative backwash on the rest of the education system"* (Oxenham 1984:220). Kohn (1993:chapters 8 and 11) provides a detailed and powerful critique of the regular use of tests and grades using research evidence to support his argument that they de-motivate pupils, harm the nature of learning that takes place, encourage cheating, damage the relationship between the teacher and learner and induce blind conformity. In a previous, and equally detailed and thoroughly researched book, Kohn (1992) set exams and testing in the wider context of the negative consequences of competition in schooling in general, arguing that competition is not an inevitable part of human nature, it harms motivation and ruins self-esteem and relationships. As a matter of principle then, all education systems need to ask which, if any, tests set by those other than learners for themselves are genuinely of benefit to the learner him or herself or really essential in some way for the wider society. At the moment many examinations administered to learners primarily serve the purposes of governments in ranking schools and even nations in league tables. Both Kohn and Oxenham include final chapters in their books on the many alternatives to existing forms of assessment but, particularly in Kohn's case, these require a re-examination of the basic purposes of education – hence the emphasis on choice, and freedom in his final chapter in the 1993 book and cooperation in the 1992 book - and a shift in thinking about and practicing education that is completely at odds with the dominant contemporary authoritarian paradigm. The current enormous over-emphasis on testing and grades gets in the way of learning and education and much of it could be scrapped tomorrow, not only with no harm to education but also with many positive benefits.

If a key aim of education is democracy and the democratic citizen, then ways of organising learning must move away from too much emphasis on the reproduction of factual learning and the 'right answer', to a greater engagement with controversy and critique. As argued above, this is not a salient feature of much contemporary schooling or teacher education, despite the potential for controversial issues arising in any area of the school curriculum or in many other aspects of school life and despite much good guidance on the principles and practice of teaching controversial issues now being in print (Advisory Group on Citizenship:1998; Carter, Harber and Serf:2003; Oxfam: 2006; Claire and Holden:2007; Harber and Serf:2007). Indeed, Davies (2008) argues that a very important strand in education for democracy is to educate against extremism, intolerance and even the terrorism it can lead to. We saw earlier in this book that education *per se* is no protection against extremism and indeed is often positively related to it. What matters is the type of education on offer. Davies emphasises the need for a human rights framework in education to provide a political education that stresses the importance of critical thinking and evaluation, of examination and discussion of alternative versions of 'truth' and taking a more nuanced look at identity. The idea is to move away from labelling of cultures, certainties and absolutes. Unfortunately, as she points out, schools currently do not, in the main, do these things, many doing the opposite by both being obsessed by testing and examinations resulting in anxiety and insecurity and condoning revenge in their punishment regimes rather than restorative justice in which offenders express remorse and make amends to the victim.

Another crucial aspect of educational change is the reform of initial teacher education in a more democratic direction. Something has got to disrupt the reproductive cycle of authoritarian school-authoritarian teacher education-authoritarian teaching to shock new teachers and open their eyes to alternatives. There have been exceptions to the authoritarian model of teacher education that have tried to provide both a critical social and political perspective on education and more democratic and participatory experiences for student teachers. Two examples from America discussed in some detail would be the University of Wisconsin, Madison (Zeichner and Liston 1987) and Indiana University at Bloomington (Beyer 2001). In Britain a democratic learning cooperative run at the University of Birmingham in the 1980s where students could write and deliver the course with tutors acting as facilitators and advisers has also been written up in some detail (Harber and Meighan 1986 and Meighan and Harber 1986). However, such courses remain in the minority and, as has been specifically pointed out by other commentators, a course such as the one run at Birmingham would be very difficult to run in contemporary Britain – even illegal - because of the increased control and regulation of teacher education (Davies, Gregory and Riley 1999:Ch. 7). In-service teacher education or continuing professional development could and should also have a significant part to play – and guidebooks on the principles and practice of democratic teacher education certainly exist (e.g. Davies, Harber and Schweisfurth:2002).

Finally, some signposts for further reading. There is a large literature on alternative forms of education, discussing not only theoretical ideas and proposals but detailing examples of working educational alternatives to authoritarian mass schooling such as democratic schools, small schools, home education and Steiner and Montessori education. Many of the sources cited below also have suggestions for further reading and contact addresses. A useful single volume overview is provided by Carnie (2003) and there are also many books and other sources of information on the website called 'The Education Revolution', which is the website of the Alternative Education Resource Organisation (http://educationrevolution.stores).

In terms of more democratic forms of education the online *Directory of Democratic Education* (http://www.democratic education.com/books.htm) is worth consulting as is the publication list of Education Heretics Press which contains a number of useful books on democratic education. Harber (1996) makes the connection between democratic education and more human scale small schools, but other useful sources on small schools are Ayers, Klonsky and Lyon (2000); the special issue of *Forum* (50,2) in 2008 on 'School Size: deepening the debate', and the website of Human Scale Education at www.hse.org.uk Interestingly, the Education section of *The Guardian Newspaper* even recently had an opinion column on the important contribution that family-like small schools can make to social cohesion (22/1/2008), indirectly, therefore, raising the opposite question of what larger, impersonal mass forms of schooling are not doing for social cohesion. Meighan (2005) also makes the connection between home-based education and a more democratic education. There has been a growing media interest in, but also a serious literature on, the area of home-based education in recent years, with it increasingly seeing it as a constructive and feasible alternative to schooling (e.g. Fortune Wood

2005, 2006 and 2007; Thomas and Pattison 2008). Further ideas and resources can be found at www.education-otherwise.org

So, and finally, there is nothing fixed or immutable about the nature of schooling. Schooling is socially and politically constructed and can be reconstructed in the direction of a more genuine education and there are many examples of, and sources on, these alternative forms of education. However, reconstruction is not necessarily an easy or comfortable task as the weight of tradition, dominant ideology, perceived 'common sense' and vested interests often have to be challenged and overcome. I expressed my doubts about being over-optimistic about genuine educational change in a progressive direction above. Sometimes, however, something happens to give one some hope. For example, in 2007 Sri Lanka, a country marked by political and ethnic violence, developed a national policy on education for social cohesion and peace, the first country that I am aware of that has an entire official education policy on peace education (Sri Lanka Ministry of Education 2007). This document recognises the need for a school culture and ethos that has a clear focus on fostering peace and respect for rights. It will be interesting to see what happens in practice. However, as one of the parents of a child at the fourth bilingual school in Israel designed to build cooperation and trust among both Arab and Israeli pupils said, *"Just because something is rare and difficult doesn't mean it's not going to work. Someone has to make start"* (McCarthy 2007). Education *can* be more democratic and geared to the promotion of human rights and the peaceful settlement of conflict and nothing is more important than this. But not in schools as they are presently constituted.

References

Adams,R. (1991) **Protests by Pupils: Empowerment, Schooling and the State** (London:Falmer Press)

Advisory Group on Citizenship (1998) **Education for Citizenship and the Teaching of Democracy in Schools** (The Crick Report) (London:Qualifications and Curriculum Authority)

Akiba,M. (2008) Predictors of Student Fear of School Violence: A Comparative Study of Eighth Graders in 3 Countries', **School Effectiveness and School Improvement** 19,1 pp51-72

Akyeampong,K. (2003) **Teacher Training in Ghana – Does it Count?** (London:DfID)

Alexander,R. (2000) **Culture and Pedagogy: International Comparisons in Primary Education** (Oxford:Blackwell)

Amnesty International (2008) **Safe Schools: Every Girl's Right** (London: Amnesty International Publications)

Apple,M. (2001) 'Markets, Standards, Teaching and Teacher Education', **Journal of Teacher Education** 52,3 pp82-96

Archer,L. and Francis,B. (2007) **Understanding Minority Ethnic Achievement** (Abingdon:Routledge)

Asthana,A. and Hinscliff,G. (2006) 'How Poor Children Miss Out on the Best Schools', **The Observer** 5/2

Ayers,W., Klonsky,M. and Lyon,G. (Eds.) (2000) **A Simple Justice : the Challenge of Small Schools** (New York:Teachers College Press)

Bartholemew,J. (1976) 'Schooling teachers : the myth of the liberal college', in G.Whitty and M.F.D. Young

(Eds.) **Explorations in the Politics of School Knowledge** (Driffield:Nafferton)

Berrebi,C. (2003) 'Evidence About the Link Between Education, Poverty and Terrorism Among Palestinians', at http://www.irs.princeton.edu/pubs/pdfs/477.pdf

Beyer,L. (2001) 'The value of critical perspectives in teacher education', **Journal of Teacher Education** 52,2 pp.151-163

Birkhead,T. (2009) 'We've bred a generation unable to think', **Times Educational Supplement** 6/2

Bloom,A. (2009) 'Inside cruel world of girl bullies', **Times Educational Supplement** 13/2

Bloom,A. (2008) 'Which Secondary? It Hardly Matters', **Times Educational Supplement** 17/10

Bloom,A. (2007) 'Staff dismiss attacks on gay pupils as teasing', **Times Educational Supplement** 29/6

Bloom,A. and Ward,H. (2008) Tests fixation sets England apart', **Times Educational Supplement** 8/2

Bosely,S. (2007) 'British children: poorer, at greater risk and more insecure', **The Guardian** 14/2

Boyle,P. (1999) **Class Formation and Civil Society: the Politics of Education in Africa** (Aldershot:Ashgate)

Brettingham,M. (2008) 'Can a 4-year-old be racist?', *The TES Magazine* 24/10

Brown,G. (2005) 'Making ethnic citizens: the politics and practice of education in Malaysia', **CRISE Working Paper 23** (Oxford:Centre for Research on Inequality, Human Security and Ethnicity)

Carnie,F. (2003) **Alternative Approaches to Education** (London:RoutledgeFalmer)

Carter,C., Harber,C. and Serf,J. (2003) **Towards Ubuntu: Critical Teacher**

Education for Democratic Citizenship in South Africa and England (Birmingham:Birmingham Development Education Centre)

Claire,H. and Holden,C (2007) **The Challenge of Teaching Controversial Issues** (Stoke on Trent:Trentham Books)

Cochran-Smith,M. (2001) **Education Policy Archives** 9,11. Online http://epaa.asu.edu/epaa/v911.html

Curtis,P. (2008a) 'Children being failed by progressive teaching, say Tories', **The Guardian** 9/5

Curtis,P. (2008b) 'Black Caribbean children held back by racism in schools, says study', **The Guardian** 5/9

Curtis,P. (2007a) 'School results still depend heavily on class', **The Guardian** 13/12

Curtis,P. (2007b) 'Study reveals stressed out 7-11 year-olds', **The Guardian** 12/10

Cushman,K. (2003) **Fires in the Bathroom** (New York:The New Press)

Davies,C. (2008) 'Most adults feel exams failed to gauge real ability', **The Observer** 7/12

Davies, I., Gregory, I. & Riley, S. (1999) **Good Citizenship and Educational Provision** (London: Falmer Press)

Davies,L. (2008) **Educating Against Extremism** (London:Trentham Books)

Davies,L., Harber,C. and Schweisfurth,M. (2002) **Democracy through Teacher Education** (Birmingham:CIER and CfBT)

Davies,L., Yamashita,H. and Harber,C. (2005**) Global Citizenship Education: the Needs of Teachers and Learners** (Birmingham: Centre for International Education and Research)

Delandshire,G. and Petrosky,A. (2004) 'Political rationales and ideological stances of the standards-

based reform of teacher education in the US',
Teaching and Teacher Education 20,1 pp1-15

Devine,D. (2003) **Children, Power and Schooling**
(Stoke on Trent:Trentham Books)

De Wet, N.C. (2007) 'Free State Educators,
Perceptions and Observations of Learner-on Learner
and Educator-on-Learner School Violence', **Education
as Change** 11,1 pp59-85

DfES (2006) **Getting it Right** (London:DfES)

Dore,R. (1976) **The Diploma Disease** (London:Allen
and Unwin)

Douse,M. (2005) 'Learning and Laughter – and let the
Livelihood Come Later', paper delivered to the 8th
UKFIET International Conference on Education and
Development, University of Oxford.

Duncan,N. (2007a) 'Bullying' in G.Richards and
F.Armstrong (Eds.) Key Issues for **Teaching
Assistants:Working in Diverse and Inclusive
Classrooms** (London:Routledge)

Duncan,N. (2007b) ''Institutional Factors in Bullying',
in I.Rivers, N.Duncan and V.E.Besag in **Bullying: A
Handbook for Educators and Parents** (Wesport
CT:Praeger)

Duncan,N. (2006) 'Gendered violence in schools', in F.
Leach and C. Mitchell (Eds.) **Combating Gender
Violence in and Around Schools (**Stoke On
Trent:Trentham Books)

Duncan,N. (1999) **Sexual Bullying**
(London:Routledge)

Elliott,J. (2007) 'From human capital theory to
capability theory as a driver of curriculum reform: a
reflection on the educational implications of the work
of Amartya Sen in the light of John Dewey's account
of educational values', in B. Somekh and T.Schwandt
(Eds.) **Knowledge Production: Research Work in
Interesting Times** (London:Routledge)

Elliott,L. (2008) 'West's pledge to tackle global poverty has been crowded out by our own crisis', **The Guardian** 1/12

Fataar,A. (2007) 'Educational renovation in a South African "township on the move": a social-spatial analysis', **International Journal of Educational Development** 27,6 pp599-612

Fiske,E. and Ladd,H. (2004) **Elusive Equity : Education reform in Post-Apartheid South Africa** (Cape Town:HSRC Press)

Fitzgerald,M. (2006) 'Japan tries to stem wave of pupil suicides', **Times Educational Supplement** 24/11

Fortune-Wood,M. (2005) **The Face of Home-Based Education 1** (Nottingham:Educational Heretics Press)

Fortune-Wood,M. (2006) **The Face of Home-Based Education 2** (Nottingham:Educational Heretics Press)

Fortune-Wood,M. (2007) **Can't Go Won't Go** (Gwynedd:Cinnamon Press)

Fox,C. and Harding,D. (2005) 'School Shootings as Organisational Deviance', **Sociology of Education** 78, pp 69-97

Francis,B. and Skelton,C. (2005) **Reassessing Gender and Achievement** (Abingdon:Routledge)

Gardiner,B. (2003) 'Foreword' to Burke,C. and Grosvenor,I. (2003) **The School that I'd Like** (London:RoutledgeFalmer)

Garner,R. and Russell,B. (2006) 'Stranglehold', **The Independent** 15/6

Gor, H. (2003) 'Education for War in Israel', in K. Saltman and D. Gabbard **Education As Enforcement: The Militarisation and Corporatisation of Schools** (New York: RoutledgeFalmer)

Gourevitch,P. (1998) **We Wish to Inform You that Tomorrow We Will be Killed with Our Families** (New York:Farrar,Strauss and Giroux)

Green,A. (1990) **Education and State Formation** (London:Macmillan)

Griffiths,V. (2000) 'The reflective dimension in teacher education', **International Journal of Educational Research** 33 pp539-555

Hallak,J. and Poisson,M. (2006) **Corrupt Schools, Corrupt Universities: What Can Be Done?** (Paris:IIEP)

Harber,C. (2009a) 'Long Time Coming: Children As Only Occasional Decision-Makers in Schools', in Còx,S., Robinson-Pant,A., Dyer,C. and Schweisfurth,M. (Eds.) **Children As Decision Makers in Education** (London:Continuum)

Harber,C. (2009b)'Revolution,What revolution? Contextual Issues in Citizenship Education in England', **Citizenship, Economic and Social Education: An International Journal** – forthcoming.

Harber,C. (2004) **Schooling As Violence** (London:RoutledgeFalmer)

Harber, C. (2001) **State of Transition: Post-Apartheid Educational Reform in South Africa** (Oxford: Symposium Books)

Harber,C. (1997) **Education, Democracy and Political Development in Africa** (Brighton:Sussex Academic Press)

Harber,C. (1996) **Small Schools and Democratic Practice** (Nottingham:Educational Heretics Press)

Harber,C. (1989) **Politics in African Education** (London:Macmillan)

Harber,C. and Davies,L. (1997) **School Management and Effectiveness in Developing Countries** (London:Cassell)

Harber,C. and Meighan,R. (1986) 'Democratic Learning in Teacher Education: a Review of Experience at one Institution', **Journal of Education for Teaching**, Vol. 12, No. 2 pp.163-72.

Harber,C. and Serf,J. (Eds.) (2007) **Comparative Education and Quality Global Learning: Engaging with Controversial Issues in South Africa and the UK** (Birmingham:Teachers in Development Education)

Harber,C. and Serf,J. (2006) 'Teacher Education for a Democratic Society in England and South Africa', **Teaching and Teacher Education** 22,8 986-997

Hartley,D. (2000) 'Shoring up the pillars of modernity : teacher education and the quest for certainty', **International Studies in the Sociology of Education** 10,2 pp113-131

Hill,A. and Hinsliff,G. (2005) 'Children's Czar Warns of Huge Leap in Bullying', **The Observer** 13/11

Holdsworth,N. (2004) 'Pupils sent to military camps', **Times Educational Supplement** 7/5

Humphreys,S. (2006) 'Corporal Punishment As Gendered Practice', in F.Leach and C. Mitchell (Eds.) **Combating Gender Violence in and Around Schools (**Stoke On Trent:Trentham Books)

Hunt,F. (2007) **Schooling Citizens: a study of policy in practice in South Africa,** Doctoral Thesis, University of Sussex

Id21 (2005) ' Making the difference: how schools influence gender identity' **Research Highlight** 25/1

Jackson,C. (2006) **Lads and Ladettes in School** (Milton Keynes:Open University Press)

Jeffrey,C., Jeffery,P. and Jeffery,R. (2008) **Degrees without Freedom: Education, Masculinities and Unemployment in North India** (Stanford University Press)

Jones,J. (1994) 'Towards an Understanding of Power Relationships in Institutional Abuse', **Early Child Development and Care** 100, pp69-76

Kaczmarek,J. (2008) 'Class of '08, spirit of 45', **The Guardian G2** 24/1

Karlsson,J. (2002) 'The Role of Democratic Governing Bodies in South African Schools', **Comparative Education** 38,3 pp327-336

Katz,A., Buchanan,A. and Bream,V. (2001) **Bullying in Britain: Testimonies from Teenagers** (East Molesey:Young Voice)

Kelly,A.V. (1986) **Knowledge and Curriculum Planning** (London:Harper and Row)

Kendall,N. (2008) ' "Vulnerability" in AIDS-affected states: Rethinking child rights, educational institutions, and the development of paradigms', **International Journal of Educational Development** 28, 4 pp365-383

Klein,J. (2006) 'Cultural capital and high school bullies', **Men and Masculinities** 9,1 pp53-75

Kohn,A. (1993) **Punished by Rewards** (Boston:Houghton Mifflin)

Kohn,A. (1992) **No Contest: the Case Against Competition** (Boston:Houghton Mifflin)

Krueger,A. and Maleckova,J. (2003) 'Education, Poverty and Terrorism : Is There a Causal Connection?', **Journal of Economic Perspectives** 4, pp119-44

Kunje,D., Lewin,K. and Stuart,J. (2003) **Primary Teacher Education in Malawi: Insights into Practice and Policy** (London:DfID)

Lall,M. (2008) 'Educate to hate : the use of education in the creation of antagonistic national identities in India and Pakistan', **Compare** 38.1 pp103-119

Lee,J. (2005) 'Worries Over Tuning in to Track Pupils', **Times Educational Supplement** 4/3

Lefoka,J. and Sebatane,E. (2003) **Initial Primary Teacher Education in Malawi** (London:DfID)

Leidig,M. (2000) 'Big Brother Tracker has Children in Sight', **Times Educational Supplement** 1/12

Loomba,A. (1998) **Colonialism/Postcolonialism** (London:Routledge)

Mangan,J.A. (Ed.) (1993) **The Imperial Curriculum: Racial Images and Education in the British Colonial Experience** (London:Routledge)

Marley,D. (2008a) 'Magic moments disappeared, experts believe', **Times Educational Supplement** 17/10

Marley,D. (2008b) 'Ofsted slams teaching to the test' *Times Educational Supplement* 25/7

Marley,D. (2007) 'From bullying to beer-drinking', **Times Educational Supplement** 16/11

Marley,D. and Hilborne,N. (2007) 'Truancy blamed on teaching', **Times Educational Supplement** 21/9

Meighan,R. (2005) **Comparing Learning Systems** (Nottingham:Educational Heretics Press)

Meighan,R. (1988) **Flexi-Schooling** (Ticknall:Education Now)

Meighan,R. (1994) **The Freethinkers' Guide to the Educational Universe** (Nottingham:Educational Heretics Press)

Meighan,R. and Harber,C. (1986) 'A Case Study of Democratic Learning in Teacher Education' **Educational Review**, Vol. 38, No. 3 pp.273-282

Meikle,J. (2007) 'Bullying: calls for national inquiry', **The Guardian** 27/3

Meyer,E. (2006) 'Gendered Harassment in North America: recognising homophobia and heterosexism among students', in F.Leach and C. Mitchell (Eds.) **Combating Gender Violence in and Around Schools (**Stoke On Trent:Trentham Books)

Milne,J. (2007) 'Pupils can be tracked round town with chips', **Times Educational Supplement** 23/11

Molteno,M., Ogadhoh,K., Cain,E. and Crumpton,B. (2000) **Towards Responsive Schools: Supporting Better Schooling for Disadvantaged Children** (London:Department for International Development/Save the Children)

Mongon,D. and Chapman,C. (2008) **Successful Leadership for Promoting the Achievement of White Working Class Pupils** (National College of School Leadership and National Union of Teachers)

Montefiore,S. (2007) 'Stalin in Love', **The Sunday Times** 6/5

Moore, K., Jones,N. and Broadbent,E. (2008) **School Violence in OECD Countries** (London : United Nations)

Moore,L. (2002) 'Scared, Not Skiving', **Guardian Education** 8/1

Moore,M. (2001) **Stupid White Men** (London:Penguin)

Nelson Mandela Foundation (2005) **Emerging Voices** (Cape Town:HSRC Press)

Niemi,H. (2002) 'Active learning – a cultural change needed in teacher education and schools', **Teaching and Teacher Education** 18, pp763-780

Northern,S. (2005) 'Enjoy an intellectual orgasm', *Times Educational Supplement* 25/2

Oliver,J. and Grimston,J. (2009) 'Milburn to tackle "elitist" professions', *The Sunday Times* 11/1

O'Malley,B. (2005) 'Heads beat to call of peace', *Times Educational Supplement* 22/7

O'Moore,M. and Minton,S. (2003) 'Tackling violence in schools: a report from Ireland', in P.Smith (Ed.) **Violence in Schools: the Response in Europe** (London:RoutledgeFalmer)

Oshako,T. (Ed.) (1997) **Violence at School: Global Issues and Interventions** (Paris:UNESCO)

Osler,A. and Starkey,H. (2005) **Changing Citizenship: Democracy and Inclusion in Education** (New York:Open University Press)

Oulton,C., Day,V., Dillon,J. and Grace,M. (2004) 'Controversial issues – teachers' attitudes and practices in the context of citizenship education', **Oxford Review of Education** 30, 4 pp490-507

Oxenham,J. (Ed.) (1984) **Education Versus Qualifications** (London:George Allen and Unwin)

Oxfam (2006) Global Citizenship Guides: Teaching Controversial Issues (Oxford:Oxfam)

Phillips,S. (2006) 'Less Tolerance for Drug Raids on Pupils', **Times Educational Supplement** 6/2

Piekarska,A. (2000) 'School Stress, Teachers' Abusive Behaviors and Children's Coping Strategies', **Child Abuse and Neglect** 24,11 pp1443-49

Pinheiro,P. (2006) **World Report on Violence Against Children** (Geneva:United Nations)

Pinker,S. (2008) **The Sexual Paradox** (New York:Simon and Schuster)

PLAN (2008) **The Global Campaign To End Violence in Schools (**Woking:PLAN)

Rahman,M. (2004a) '78 Children Die as Fire Sweeps School in India', **The Guardian** 17/7

Rahman,M. (2004b) 'Schools Ordered to Close in Wake of Indian Fire Deaths', **The Guardian** 19/7

Richardson,C. (2004) 'After School Clubs', **The Guardian** 15/11

Rimer,S. (2004) 'Unruly Students As Delinquents', **International Herald Tribune** 5/1

Roland,E. and Munthe,E. (1989) **Bullying: An International Perspective** (London:David Fulton)

Rousmaniere,K., Dehli,K. and de Conink-Smith,N. (1997) **Discipline, Moral Regulation and Schooling** (New York:Garland)

Ruiz,R.O. (1998) 'Indiscipline or violence? The problem of bullying in school', **Prospects** XVIII, No. 4 pp.587-599

Russell,B. (1926) **On Education, Especially in Early Childhood** (London:George Allen and Unwin)

Saltman.K. and Gabbard,D. (2003**) Education As Enforcement: The Militarisation and Corporatisation of Schools** (New York: RoutledgeFalmer)

Save The Children (2006) 'Save the Children: Mongolia to Protect over 650,000 Children' (www.politics.co.uk/press-releases/domestic-policy,children/child-abuse/save-ch)

Schweisfurth,M. (2002) 'Democracy and Teacher Education: negotiating practice in The Gambia', **Comparative Education** 38,3 pp 303-314

Sen,A. (1999) **Development As Freedom** (Oxford:Oxford University Press)

Shariff,S. (2008) **Cyber-Bullying** (Abingdon:Routledge)

Slater,J. (2005) 'Behaviour: are you winning?', **Times Educational Supplement** 4/3

Smith,P. (2005) **BPS Seminar Series on Bullying** (London:Goldsmiths College)

Smith,P. and Ananiadou,K. (2003) 'The Nature of School Bullying and the Effectiveness of School-Based Interventions', **Journal of Applied Psychoanalytic Studies** 5,2 pp189-209

Soudien,C. (2007) 'The "A" factor: coming to terms with the question of legacy in South African education', **International Journal of Educational Development** 27,2 pp182-193

Sri Lanka Ministry of Education (2007) **Education for Social Cohesion and Peace: A Comprehensive Framework for a National Policy** (Columbo)

Stanbrook,P. (2002) **The Whistleblowers** (Nottingham:Education Now)

Sultana,R. (2006) **Facing the Hidden Drop-Out Challenge in Albania** (Tirana:UNICEF)

Tafa,E. (2002) 'Corporal Punishment : The Brutal Face of Botswana's Authoritarian Schools', **Educational Review** 54,1 pp.17-26

Taylor,M. (2006) 'It's Official: Class Matters', **Education Guardian** 28/2

Taylor,M. (2005) 'Schools Accused of Abandoning Thousands of Gay Children to Classroom Bullies', **The Guardian** 9/5

Teeka-Bhattarai,S. (2006) 'Corporal Punishment in Schools : Issues, Efforts and Experiences with Children's Clubs in Nepal', Paper delivered at ESRC Seminar on Children As Decision-Makers, University of East Anglia.

Thomas,A. and Pattison,H. (2008) **How Children Learn at Home** (London:Continuum)

Traynor,I. (2007) 'Apartheid in the heart of Europe: how Roma children lose out on education', **The Guardian** 16/11

UNESCO (2009) **Education for All Global Monitoring Report Overcoming Inequality: Why Governance Matters** (Paris:UNESCO)

UNESCO (2008) **Education for All by 2015: will we make it? EFA Global Monitoring Report** (Paris:UNESCO)

UNESCO (2003) **Education Today** No.4 January-March

UNESCO (1989) **Seville Statement on Violence** (www.unesco.org/human_rights/hrfv.htm)

Vally,S. and Dalamba,Y. (1999) **Racism, 'Racial Integration' and Desegregation in South African Public Secondary Schools** (Johannesburg:South African Human Rights Commission)

Ward,L. (2007) 'Almost all children aged 10-15 are victims of crime', **The Guardian** 10/10

Watkins,K. (1999) **Education Now: Break the Cycle of Poverty** (Oxford:Oxfam)

Webster,M. (Ed.) (2008) **Personalised Learning** (Nottingham:Educational Heretics Press)

Whitted,K. and Dupper,D. (2008) 'Do Teachers Bully Students?', **Education and Urban Society** 40,3 pp329-41

WHO (World Health Organisation) (2002) **World Report on Violence and Health** (Geneva:WHO)

Wibowo,R. (2005) **Do Adults Listen to Children's Voices?** Unpublished Ed.D Thesis, University of Birmingham

Williams,E. (2005) 'Shadow of abuse lingers over abbey', **Times Educational Supplement** 25/11

Yoneyama,S. (2000) 'Student Discourse on Tokokjohi (School Phobia/Refusal) in Japan: burnout or empowerment?', **British Journal of Sociology of Education** 21,1 pp77-94

Zdravomyslova,O. and Gorshkova,I. (2006) 'The Usual Evil: gender violence in Russian schools', in F.Leach and C. Mitchell (Eds.) **Combating Gender Violence in and Around Schools (**Stoke On Trent:Trentham Books)

Zeichner,K. and Liston,D. (1987) 'Teaching student teachers to reflect', **Harvard Educational Review** 57,1 pp23-48

Further reading

Adcock, J. (2000) **Teaching Tomorrow**
(Nottingham: Education Now Books)

Gatto, J. T. (2009) **Weapons of Mass Instruction**
(British Columbia: New Society Publications)

Glines, D. (1995) **Creating Alternative Futures**
(Michigan: McNaughton and Gunn)

Harber, C. (2004) **Schooling as Violence**
(London: Routledge Falmer)

Holt, J. (1977) **Instead of Education**
(Harmondsworth: Penguin)

Husen, T. (1974) **The Learning Society**
(London: Methuen)

Kohl, H (1970) **The Open Classroom**
(London: Methuen)

Meighan, R. (2005) **Comparing Learning Systems**
(Nottingham:Educational Heretics Press)

Meighan, R. (2002) **John Holt: Personalised
learning instead of 'univited teaching'**
(Nottingham: Educational Heretics Press)

Priesnitz, W. (2009) **Life Learning, lessons from
the educational   frontier**
(Toronto: The Alternative Press)

Mark Vaughn, Tim Brighouse, A.S.Neill, Zoe Neill
Redhead and Ian Stonach, **Summerhill and A.S.Neill**
(Maidenhead: Open University Press)